50 German Pizza Recipes for Home

By: Kelly Johnson

Table of Contents

Classic German Pizza Recipes:

- Sausage and Sauerkraut Pizza
- Bavarian Pretzel Pizza
- Wiener Schnitzel Pizza
- Kartoffelpuffer (Potato Pancake) Pizza
- German BBQ Chicken Pizza
- Königsberger Klopse Pizza
- Zwiebelkuchen (Onion Pie) Pizza
- Bratkartoffeln (Fried Potatoes) Pizza
- Mettbrötchen Pizza
- German Cheese Spaetzle Pizza
- Rinderrouladen Pizza
- Gurkensalat (Cucumber Salad) Pizza
- Linsensuppe (Lentil Soup) Pizza
- Schweinshaxe Pizza
- Krautwickel (Cabbage Rolls) Pizza

Seasonal and Regional Varieties:

- Asparagus and Ham Pizza
- Chanterelle Mushroom Pizza
- German Apple Strudel Pizza
- Cabbage and Bacon Pizza
- White Asparagus and Smoked Salmon Pizza
- White Asparagus and Ham Hock Pizza
- Rübenkraut (Turnip Greens) and Bacon Pizza
- Bayrischer Wurstsalat (Bavarian Sausage Salad) Pizza
- Kartoffelsalat (Potato Salad) Pizza
- Blaubeerpfannkuchen (Blueberry Pancake) Dessert Pizza
- Käsespätzle and Apple Pizza
- Brezenknödel (Pretzel Dumpling) Pizza
- Pflaumenkuchen (Plum Cake) Dessert Pizza
- Weißwurst (White Sausage) and Mustard Pizza
- Grünkohl (Kale) and Smoked Pork Pizza

Fusion and Creative Varieties:

- Currywurst Pizza
- German Beer Cheese and Brat Pizza
- Black Forest Cherry Chocolate Pizza
- Pretzel Crust Schnitzel Pizza
- Rote Grütze Dessert Pizza
- Käsespätzle Pizza
- Apfelstrudel Pizza
- Döner Kebab Pizza
- Sauerbraten Pizza
- German Curry Pizza

Vegetarian and Vegan Options:

- German Potato Salad Pizza
- Vegan Sauerkraut and Tempeh Pizza
- Spargel (White Asparagus) and Hollandaise Pizza
- German-style Zucchini and Leek Pizza
- Vegan Black Forest Pizza
- Vegan Kartoffelsuppe Pizza
- Vegan Rösti Pizza
- Vegan Apfelkuchen (Apple Cake) Dessert Pizza
- Vegan Sauerkraut and Potato Pizza
- Vegan Schwarzwälder Kirschtorte Pizza

Classic German Pizza Recipes:

Sausage and Sauerkraut Pizza

Ingredients:

For the Pizza:

- 1 pizza dough (store-bought or homemade)
- 1/2 cup tomato sauce
- 1 1/2 cups shredded mozzarella cheese
- 1 cup sauerkraut, drained
- 1/2 pound German sausage (such as bratwurst or knockwurst), cooked and sliced
- 1 tablespoon whole grain mustard
- Salt and pepper to taste
- Fresh parsley, chopped (for garnish)

Optional Toppings:

- Sliced red onions
- Caraway seeds

Instructions:

Preheat Oven:
- Preheat your oven according to the pizza dough package instructions.

Roll Out Pizza Dough:
- Roll out the pizza dough on a floured surface to your desired thickness.

Assemble Pizza:
- Place the rolled-out dough on a pizza stone or baking sheet.
- Spread a layer of tomato sauce evenly over the dough, leaving a small border around the edges.
- Sprinkle shredded mozzarella cheese over the sauce.
- Distribute sauerkraut and sliced German sausage evenly over the cheese.
- Optional: Add sliced red onions for extra flavor.
- Drizzle whole grain mustard over the toppings.
- Season with salt and pepper to taste.

Bake:
- Follow the pizza dough package instructions for baking. Typically, bake in a preheated oven until the crust is golden, and the cheese is melted and bubbly.

Garnish:
- Once out of the oven, sprinkle with caraway seeds (optional) and chopped fresh parsley for a burst of freshness.

Serve:
- Slice the Sausage and Sauerkraut Pizza into portions and serve hot.

Enjoy the wonderful combination of savory sausage, tangy sauerkraut, and the zing of mustard on your pizza! Feel free to customize with additional toppings or adjust the quantities to suit your taste.

Bavarian Pretzel Pizza

Ingredients:

For the Pretzel Crust:

- 1 pizza dough (store-bought or homemade)
- 1 cup warm water (110°F/43°C)
- 1 tablespoon sugar
- 2 1/4 teaspoons active dry yeast
- 3 cups all-purpose flour
- 1 teaspoon salt
- 2 tablespoons baking soda
- Coarse sea salt for sprinkling

For the Pizza:

- 2 tablespoons Dijon mustard
- 2 cups shredded Gruyere or Swiss cheese
- 1 cup sliced bratwurst or your favorite German sausage
- 1/2 cup caramelized onions
- Chopped fresh chives for garnish (optional)

Instructions:

For the Pretzel Crust:

Activate Yeast:
- In a bowl, combine warm water, sugar, and active dry yeast. Let it sit for about 5-10 minutes until it becomes frothy.

Mix Dough:
- In a large mixing bowl, combine flour and salt. Pour in the activated yeast mixture and mix until a dough forms.
- Knead the dough on a floured surface until it becomes smooth. Place it back in the bowl, cover, and let it rise for about 1 hour or until doubled in size.

Preheat Oven:
- Preheat your oven to 475°F (245°C). If you have a pizza stone, place it in the oven to heat.

Shape the Crust:
- Punch down the dough and divide it in half. Roll out each portion into a circle, creating your pizza crust.

Boil Dough:

- In a large pot, bring water and baking soda to a boil. Boil each pizza crust for about 30 seconds on each side. Remove and let excess water drip off.

Bake:
- If using a pizza stone, transfer the crust onto a pizza peel or an inverted baking sheet dusted with flour or cornmeal.
- Spread Dijon mustard over the crust, leaving a small border around the edges.
- Sprinkle shredded Gruyere or Swiss cheese evenly over the mustard.
- Top with sliced bratwurst and caramelized onions.
- Sprinkle coarse sea salt over the toppings.
- Bake in the preheated oven for about 12-15 minutes or until the crust is golden and the cheese is melted and bubbly.

Garnish:
- Garnish with chopped fresh chives if desired.

Serve:
- Slice the Bavarian Pretzel Pizza into portions and serve hot.

Enjoy the delightful fusion of soft pretzel flavors and classic pizza toppings with this Bavarian Pretzel Pizza! Adjust the toppings and quantities according to your preferences.

Wiener Schnitzel Pizza

Ingredients:

For the Wiener Schnitzel:

- 4 boneless and thin veal or pork cutlets
- Salt and pepper to taste
- 1 cup all-purpose flour
- 2 large eggs, beaten
- 1 cup breadcrumbs (preferably Panko)
- Vegetable oil for frying
- Lemon wedges for serving

For the Pizza:

- 1 pizza dough (store-bought or homemade)
- 1/2 cup mayonnaise
- 1 tablespoon Dijon mustard
- 1 1/2 cups shredded mozzarella cheese
- 1/2 cup pickles, sliced
- Fresh parsley, chopped (for garnish)
- Lemon wedges for serving

Instructions:

For the Wiener Schnitzel:

Prepare Cutlets:
- Season the veal or pork cutlets with salt and pepper.

Breading Process:
- Set up a breading station with three shallow bowls: one with flour, one with beaten eggs, and one with breadcrumbs.
- Dredge each cutlet in flour, then dip in the beaten eggs, and coat with breadcrumbs, pressing the breadcrumbs onto the cutlets to adhere.

Fry Schnitzel:
- In a large skillet, heat vegetable oil over medium-high heat.
- Fry the breaded cutlets until golden brown and cooked through, about 3-4 minutes per side.
- Place the schnitzel on a paper towel-lined plate to drain excess oil.

Slice and Serve:

- Slice the Wiener Schnitzel into strips and serve with lemon wedges.

For the Pizza:

Preheat Oven:
- Preheat your oven according to the pizza dough package instructions.

Roll Out Pizza Dough:
- Roll out the pizza dough on a floured surface to your desired thickness.

Mix Sauce:
- In a small bowl, mix mayonnaise and Dijon mustard to create the sauce.

Assemble Pizza:
- Place the rolled-out dough on a pizza stone or baking sheet.
- Spread the mayonnaise and Dijon mustard sauce evenly over the dough, leaving a small border around the edges.
- Sprinkle shredded mozzarella cheese over the sauce.
- Arrange the sliced Wiener Schnitzel and pickles evenly over the cheese.

Bake:
- Follow the pizza dough package instructions for baking. Typically, bake in a preheated oven until the crust is golden, and the cheese is melted and bubbly.

Garnish:
- Sprinkle chopped fresh parsley over the baked pizza.

Serve:
- Slice the Wiener Schnitzel Pizza into portions and serve hot, accompanied by lemon wedges.

Enjoy the unique and delicious combination of Wiener Schnitzel flavors on your pizza! Customize with additional toppings or drizzle extra Dijon mustard for an added burst of taste.

Kartoffelpuffer (Potato Pancake) Pizza

Ingredients:

For the Potato Pancake Crust:

- 4 medium-sized potatoes, peeled and grated
- 1 small onion, finely grated
- 2 eggs, beaten
- 2 tablespoons all-purpose flour
- Salt and pepper to taste
- 2 tablespoons vegetable oil

For the Pizza Toppings:

- 1 cup sour cream
- 1 cup applesauce
- 1 cup shredded Gouda or Emmental cheese
- 4 slices cooked bacon, crumbled
- Chives, chopped (for garnish)

Instructions:

For the Potato Pancake Crust:

Prepare Potato Pancake Mixture:
- In a large bowl, combine grated potatoes and finely grated onions. Place the mixture in a clean kitchen towel and squeeze out excess moisture.
- Return the mixture to the bowl and add beaten eggs, all-purpose flour, salt, and pepper. Mix well.

Cook Potato Pancake Crust:
- Heat vegetable oil in a large skillet over medium heat.
- Spread the potato mixture evenly in the skillet, pressing it down to form a round crust.
- Cook until the edges are golden brown, then carefully flip and cook the other side until crispy. Remove from the skillet.

Preheat Oven:
- Preheat your oven according to the pizza dough package instructions.

Roll Out Pizza Dough:
- Roll out the pizza dough on a floured surface to your desired thickness.

Assemble Pizza:

- Place the rolled-out dough on a pizza stone or baking sheet.
- Carefully transfer the cooked potato pancake to the pizza dough, creating a crust.
- Spread sour cream over the potato crust.
- Sprinkle shredded Gouda or Emmental cheese evenly over the sour cream.
- Distribute crumbled bacon over the cheese.

Bake:
- Follow the pizza dough package instructions for baking. Typically, bake in a preheated oven until the crust is golden, and the cheese is melted and bubbly.

Garnish:
- Drizzle applesauce over the baked pizza.
- Sprinkle chopped chives over the top.

Serve:
- Slice the Kartoffelpuffer Pizza into portions and serve hot.

Enjoy the unique combination of crispy potato pancake crust with savory toppings on your pizza! Customize with additional toppings or adjust the quantities to suit your taste.

German BBQ Chicken Pizza

Ingredients:

For the BBQ Chicken:

- 2 boneless, skinless chicken breasts
- Salt and pepper to taste
- 1 cup barbecue sauce
- 1 tablespoon Dijon mustard
- 1 tablespoon honey
- 1 teaspoon smoked paprika
- 1 teaspoon garlic powder
- 1/2 teaspoon onion powder
- Vegetable oil for grilling

For the Pizza:

- 1 pizza dough (store-bought or homemade)
- 1/2 cup barbecue sauce
- 1 1/2 cups shredded mozzarella cheese
- 1 cup red cabbage, thinly sliced
- 1/2 red onion, thinly sliced
- 2 tablespoons fresh cilantro, chopped (for garnish)
- Lemon wedges (for serving)

Instructions:

For the BBQ Chicken:

Season and Grill Chicken:
- Season chicken breasts with salt and pepper.
- Preheat the grill or grill pan over medium-high heat.
- Grill chicken until fully cooked, with nice grill marks.
- In a bowl, mix barbecue sauce, Dijon mustard, honey, smoked paprika, garlic powder, and onion powder.
- Brush the barbecue mixture over the grilled chicken in the last few minutes of cooking.

Shred Chicken:
- Remove chicken from the grill and let it rest for a few minutes.
- Shred the chicken using two forks.

For the Pizza:

- Preheat Oven:
  - Preheat your oven according to the pizza dough package instructions.
- Roll Out Pizza Dough:
  - Roll out the pizza dough on a floured surface to your desired thickness.
- Assemble Pizza:
  - Place the rolled-out dough on a pizza stone or baking sheet.
  - Spread barbecue sauce evenly over the dough, leaving a small border around the edges.
  - Sprinkle shredded mozzarella cheese over the sauce.
  - Distribute shredded BBQ chicken, sliced red cabbage, and sliced red onion evenly over the cheese.
- Bake:
  - Follow the pizza dough package instructions for baking. Typically, bake in a preheated oven until the crust is golden, and the cheese is melted and bubbly.
- Garnish:
  - Sprinkle chopped fresh cilantro over the baked pizza.
- Serve:
  - Slice the German BBQ Chicken Pizza into portions and serve hot.
  - Optionally, serve with lemon wedges on the side for an extra burst of freshness.

Enjoy the savory and smoky flavors of German BBQ Chicken on your pizza! Customize with additional toppings or drizzle extra barbecue sauce for added flavor.

Königsberger Klopse Pizza

Ingredients:

For the Königsberger Klopse:

- 1 pound ground veal or a mix of veal and pork
- 1/2 cup breadcrumbs
- 1/4 cup milk
- 1 small onion, finely minced
- 2 tablespoons capers, drained and chopped
- 1 tablespoon Dijon mustard
- 1 tablespoon fresh parsley, chopped
- Salt and pepper to taste
- 2 tablespoons vegetable oil for frying

For the Pizza:

- 1 pizza dough (store-bought or homemade)
- 1/2 cup white sauce or béchamel sauce
- 1 cup shredded Gruyere or Emmental cheese
- 1/4 cup capers
- Fresh parsley, chopped (for garnish)
- Lemon wedges (for serving)

Instructions:

For the Königsberger Klopse:

Prepare Königsberger Klopse Mixture:
- In a bowl, combine ground veal (or veal and pork mix), breadcrumbs, milk, minced onion, chopped capers, Dijon mustard, chopped parsley, salt, and pepper. Mix until well combined.
- Shape the mixture into small meatballs.

Cook Königsberger Klopse:
- In a large skillet, heat vegetable oil over medium heat.
- Fry the meatballs until they are cooked through and have a golden brown exterior. Remove from the skillet and set aside.

For the Pizza:

Preheat Oven:
- Preheat your oven according to the pizza dough package instructions.

Roll Out Pizza Dough:
- Roll out the pizza dough on a floured surface to your desired thickness.

Assemble Pizza:
- Place the rolled-out dough on a pizza stone or baking sheet.
- Spread white sauce or béchamel sauce evenly over the dough, leaving a small border around the edges.
- Sprinkle shredded Gruyere or Emmental cheese evenly over the sauce.
- Arrange the cooked Königsberger Klopse and capers evenly over the cheese.

Bake:
- Follow the pizza dough package instructions for baking. Typically, bake in a preheated oven until the crust is golden, and the cheese is melted and bubbly.

Garnish:
- Sprinkle chopped fresh parsley over the baked pizza.

Serve:
- Slice the Königsberger Klopse Pizza into portions and serve hot.
- Optionally, serve with lemon wedges on the side for an extra burst of freshness.

Enjoy the unique and savory taste of Königsberger Klopse on your pizza! Customize with additional toppings or drizzle extra white sauce for added flavor.

Zwiebelkuchen (Onion Pie) Pizza

Ingredients:

For the Onion Pie Filling:

- 4 large onions, thinly sliced
- 2 tablespoons butter
- 2 tablespoons all-purpose flour
- 1 cup sour cream
- 2 large eggs
- Salt and pepper to taste
- 1/2 teaspoon caraway seeds (optional)

For the Pizza:

- 1 pizza dough (store-bought or homemade)
- 1 cup shredded Gruyere or Emmental cheese
- Fresh thyme leaves (for garnish)
- Crispy bacon bits (optional)

Instructions:

For the Onion Pie Filling:

Caramelize Onions:
- In a large skillet, melt butter over medium heat. Add thinly sliced onions and cook, stirring occasionally, until they become soft and caramelized, about 15-20 minutes.

Prepare Custard Filling:
- Sprinkle flour over the caramelized onions and stir to coat.
- In a bowl, whisk together sour cream, eggs, salt, pepper, and caraway seeds if using.
- Pour the sour cream mixture over the onions and stir until well combined. Cook for an additional 2-3 minutes until the filling thickens slightly.

For the Pizza:

Preheat Oven:
- Preheat your oven according to the pizza dough package instructions.

Roll Out Pizza Dough:
- Roll out the pizza dough on a floured surface to your desired thickness.

Assemble Pizza:
- Place the rolled-out dough on a pizza stone or baking sheet.
- Spread the prepared onion pie filling evenly over the dough, leaving a small border around the edges.
- Sprinkle shredded Gruyere or Emmental cheese evenly over the filling.

Bake:
- Follow the pizza dough package instructions for baking. Typically, bake in a preheated oven until the crust is golden, and the cheese is melted and bubbly.

Garnish:
- Sprinkle fresh thyme leaves over the baked pizza.
- Optionally, add crispy bacon bits for extra flavor.

Serve:
- Slice the Zwiebelkuchen Pizza into portions and serve hot.

Enjoy the delicious fusion of Zwiebelkuchen flavors on your pizza! The creamy onion custard filling combined with the melted cheese creates a savory and comforting dish. Customize with additional toppings or herbs to suit your taste.

Bratkartoffeln (Fried Potatoes) Pizza

Ingredients:

For the Bratkartoffeln:

- 4 medium-sized potatoes, peeled and thinly sliced
- 1 large onion, finely chopped
- 4 slices bacon, diced
- 2 tablespoons vegetable oil
- Salt and pepper to taste
- Chopped fresh parsley for garnish

For the Pizza:

- 1 pizza dough (store-bought or homemade)
- 1 cup crème fraîche or sour cream
- 1 cup shredded Gouda cheese
- 1/2 cup sautéed mushrooms (optional)
- Chives, chopped (for garnish)

Instructions:

For the Bratkartoffeln:

　Precook Potatoes:
- Parboil the thinly sliced potatoes in salted water for about 5 minutes until slightly tender. Drain and set aside.

　Cook Potatoes and Bacon:
- In a large skillet, heat vegetable oil over medium heat. Add chopped onions and diced bacon, and cook until the bacon is crispy and the onions are golden.

　Fry Potatoes:
- Add the parboiled potatoes to the skillet, spreading them out in a single layer. Allow them to cook without stirring for a few minutes until they form a golden crust. Then, flip and cook the other side until golden and crispy.
- Season with salt and pepper to taste. Sprinkle chopped fresh parsley over the potatoes. Set aside.

For the Pizza:

Preheat Oven:
- Preheat your oven according to the pizza dough package instructions.

Roll Out Pizza Dough:
- Roll out the pizza dough on a floured surface to your desired thickness.

Assemble Pizza:
- Place the rolled-out dough on a pizza stone or baking sheet.
- Spread crème fraîche or sour cream evenly over the dough, leaving a small border around the edges.
- Sprinkle shredded Gouda cheese evenly over the cream.

Add Fried Potatoes:
- Distribute the Bratkartoffeln (fried potatoes) evenly over the cheese.
- Optionally, add sautéed mushrooms for extra flavor.

Bake:
- Follow the pizza dough package instructions for baking. Typically, bake in a preheated oven until the crust is golden, and the cheese is melted and bubbly.

Garnish:
- Sprinkle chopped chives over the baked pizza.

Serve:
- Slice the Bratkartoffeln Pizza into portions and serve hot.

Enjoy the comforting and hearty flavors of Bratkartoffeln on your pizza! Customize with additional toppings or herbs to suit your taste.

Mettbrötchen Pizza

Ingredients:

For the Mettbrötchen Topping:

- 1/2 pound high-quality minced pork
- 1 small onion, finely chopped
- 2 tablespoons fresh parsley, chopped
- Salt and pepper to taste
- 1 teaspoon Dijon mustard (optional)
- 1 tablespoon vegetable oil

For the Pizza:

- 1 pizza dough (store-bought or homemade)
- 2 tablespoons crème fraîche or sour cream
- 1 cup arugula (rocket), washed and dried
- 1 tablespoon capers, drained
- Fresh chives, chopped (for garnish)

Instructions:

For the Mettbrötchen Topping:

Prepare Minced Pork:
- In a bowl, combine minced pork, finely chopped onion, chopped parsley, salt, pepper, and Dijon mustard (if using).
- Mix well to evenly distribute the seasonings.

Cook Minced Pork:
- Heat vegetable oil in a skillet over medium heat.
- Add the seasoned minced pork mixture to the skillet and cook for a few minutes until the pork is browned. Ensure it's fully cooked to eliminate any safety concerns associated with raw meat.

For the Pizza:

Preheat Oven:
- Preheat your oven according to the pizza dough package instructions.

Roll Out Pizza Dough:
- Roll out the pizza dough on a floured surface to your desired thickness.

Assemble Pizza:

- Place the rolled-out dough on a pizza stone or baking sheet.
- Spread crème fraîche or sour cream evenly over the dough, leaving a small border around the edges.
- Distribute the cooked minced pork mixture evenly over the cream.

Add Fresh Toppings:
- Scatter arugula (rocket) over the pizza.
- Sprinkle capers over the top.

Bake:
- Follow the pizza dough package instructions for baking. Typically, bake in a preheated oven until the crust is golden, and the toppings are heated through.

Garnish:
- Sprinkle chopped fresh chives over the baked pizza.

Serve:
- Slice the Mettbrötchen Pizza into portions and serve hot.

Enjoy the unique combination of flavors inspired by Mettbrötchen on your pizza! Customize with additional toppings or herbs to suit your taste.

German Cheese Spaetzle Pizza

Ingredients:

For the Spaetzle:

- 2 cups all-purpose flour
- 4 large eggs
- 1/2 cup milk
- 1/2 teaspoon salt
- 1/4 teaspoon ground nutmeg

For the Pizza:

- 1 pizza dough (store-bought or homemade)
- 1 cup grated Emmental cheese
- 1 cup grated Gruyere cheese
- 1/2 cup caramelized onions
- 2 tablespoons butter
- Chopped fresh chives for garnish

Instructions:

For the Spaetzle:

Prepare Spaetzle Dough:
- In a bowl, whisk together flour, eggs, milk, salt, and nutmeg until you have a smooth batter.

Cook Spaetzle:
- Bring a large pot of salted water to a boil.
- Using a spaetzle maker or a colander with large holes, press the batter through into the boiling water. Cook for about 2-3 minutes or until the spaetzle floats to the surface.
- Remove the spaetzle with a slotted spoon and transfer to a bowl.

Saute Spaetzle:
- In a skillet, melt 2 tablespoons of butter over medium heat. Add the cooked spaetzle and sauté until they are lightly browned.

For the Pizza:

Preheat Oven:
- Preheat your oven according to the pizza dough package instructions.

Roll Out Pizza Dough:
- Roll out the pizza dough on a floured surface to your desired thickness.

Assemble Pizza:
- Place the rolled-out dough on a pizza stone or baking sheet.
- Spread the sautéed spaetzle evenly over the dough, leaving a small border around the edges.
- Sprinkle a mixture of grated Emmental and Gruyere cheese evenly over the spaetzle.
- Distribute caramelized onions over the cheese.

Bake:
- Follow the pizza dough package instructions for baking. Typically, bake in a preheated oven until the crust is golden, and the cheese is melted and bubbly.

Garnish:
- Sprinkle chopped fresh chives over the baked pizza.

Serve:
- Slice the German Cheese Spaetzle Pizza into portions and serve hot.

Enjoy the delicious combination of cheesy spaetzle on your pizza! Customize with additional toppings or herbs to suit your taste.

Rinderrouladen Pizza

Ingredients:

For the Rinderrouladen-inspired Filling:

- 4 beef sirloin or flank steak slices (about 1/4 inch thick)
- Dijon mustard
- Salt and pepper to taste
- 4 slices bacon
- 1 large onion, finely chopped
- 4 large pickles, sliced into thin strips
- Vegetable oil for cooking

For the Pizza:

- 1 pizza dough (store-bought or homemade)
- 1/2 cup crème fraîche or sour cream
- 1 cup shredded Gouda cheese
- 2 tablespoons whole-grain mustard
- Chopped fresh parsley for garnish

Instructions:

For the Rinderrouladen-inspired Filling:

Prepare Beef Slices:
- Pound the beef slices to an even thickness.
- Spread a thin layer of Dijon mustard over each beef slice. Season with salt and pepper.

Cook Bacon and Onions:
- In a skillet, cook bacon until crispy. Remove bacon from the skillet and set it aside.
- In the same skillet, using the bacon fat, sauté finely chopped onions until golden.

Assemble Rinderrouladen Filling:
- Lay out the beef slices. Place a slice of cooked bacon and a portion of sautéed onions on each slice.
- Add strips of pickles on top of the bacon and onions.
- Roll up each beef slice, securing them with toothpicks if needed.

Cook Rinderrouladen:
- In the same skillet, heat vegetable oil over medium-high heat.
- Brown the Rinderrouladen on all sides, ensuring they are cooked through.

For the Pizza:

- Preheat Oven:
  - Preheat your oven according to the pizza dough package instructions.
- Roll Out Pizza Dough:
  - Roll out the pizza dough on a floured surface to your desired thickness.
- Assemble Pizza:
  - Place the rolled-out dough on a pizza stone or baking sheet.
  - Spread crème fraîche or sour cream evenly over the dough, leaving a small border around the edges.
  - Sprinkle shredded Gouda cheese evenly over the cream.
  - Distribute the cooked Rinderrouladen over the cheese.
  - Drizzle whole-grain mustard over the top.
- Bake:
  - Follow the pizza dough package instructions for baking. Typically, bake in a preheated oven until the crust is golden, and the cheese is melted and bubbly.
- Garnish:
  - Sprinkle chopped fresh parsley over the baked pizza.
- Serve:
  - Slice the Rinderrouladen Pizza into portions and serve hot.

Enjoy the unique and savory flavors of Rinderrouladen on your pizza! Customize with additional toppings or herbs to suit your taste.

Gurkensalat (Cucumber Salad) Pizza

Ingredients:

For the Cucumber Salad:

- 2 large cucumbers, thinly sliced
- 1/2 red onion, thinly sliced
- 1/4 cup chopped fresh dill
- 1/2 cup white vinegar
- 1/4 cup water
- 2 tablespoons sugar
- Salt and pepper to taste

For the Pizza:

- 1 pizza dough (store-bought or homemade)
- 1/2 cup cream cheese or Greek yogurt
- 1 cup shredded smoked salmon (or your preferred smoked fish)
- 1 tablespoon capers, drained
- Lemon zest (from one lemon)
- Fresh chives, chopped (for garnish)

Instructions:

For the Cucumber Salad:

Prepare Cucumber Salad:
- In a bowl, combine thinly sliced cucumbers, thinly sliced red onion, and chopped fresh dill.

Make Dressing:
- In a separate bowl, whisk together white vinegar, water, sugar, salt, and pepper until the sugar dissolves.
- Pour the dressing over the cucumber mixture and toss to coat.
- Refrigerate the cucumber salad for at least 30 minutes to allow the flavors to meld.

For the Pizza:

Preheat Oven:
- Preheat your oven according to the pizza dough package instructions.

Roll Out Pizza Dough:

- Roll out the pizza dough on a floured surface to your desired thickness.

Assemble Pizza:
- Place the rolled-out dough on a pizza stone or baking sheet.
- Spread cream cheese or Greek yogurt evenly over the dough, leaving a small border around the edges.
- Distribute the marinated cucumber salad evenly over the cream.
- Sprinkle shredded smoked salmon over the cucumber salad.
- Scatter capers over the top.
- Zest a lemon over the pizza.

Bake:
- Follow the pizza dough package instructions for baking. Typically, bake in a preheated oven until the crust is golden, and the toppings are heated through.

Garnish:
- Sprinkle chopped fresh chives over the baked pizza.

Serve:
- Slice the Gurkensalat Pizza into portions and serve hot.

Enjoy the refreshing and unique combination of Gurkensalat flavors on your pizza! Customize with additional toppings or herbs to suit your taste.

Linsensuppe (Lentil Soup) Pizza

Ingredients:

For the Lentil Soup Base:

- 1 cup dried green or brown lentils, rinsed and drained
- 1 onion, finely chopped
- 2 carrots, diced
- 2 celery stalks, diced
- 3 cloves garlic, minced
- 1 can (14 oz) diced tomatoes
- 4 cups vegetable broth
- 1 teaspoon ground cumin
- 1 teaspoon ground coriander
- 1/2 teaspoon smoked paprika
- Salt and pepper to taste
- 2 tablespoons olive oil

For the Pizza:

- 1 pizza dough (store-bought or homemade)
- 1 cup shredded mozzarella cheese
- 1/2 cup crumbled feta cheese
- Fresh parsley, chopped (for garnish)
- Lemon wedges (for serving)

Instructions:

For the Lentil Soup Base:

Prepare Lentil Soup:
- In a large pot, heat olive oil over medium heat. Add chopped onion, carrots, celery, and garlic. Sauté until vegetables are softened.
- Add rinsed lentils, diced tomatoes, vegetable broth, ground cumin, ground coriander, smoked paprika, salt, and pepper. Bring to a boil, then reduce heat and simmer until lentils are tender, about 20-25 minutes.

Blend Soup:
- Using an immersion blender, partially blend the soup to achieve a chunky consistency. Alternatively, blend a portion of the soup in a blender and return it to the pot.

For the Pizza:

- Preheat Oven:
    - Preheat your oven according to the pizza dough package instructions.
- Roll Out Pizza Dough:
    - Roll out the pizza dough on a floured surface to your desired thickness.
- Assemble Pizza:
    - Place the rolled-out dough on a pizza stone or baking sheet.
    - Spread a layer of the lentil soup base evenly over the dough, leaving a small border around the edges.
    - Sprinkle shredded mozzarella cheese and crumbled feta cheese evenly over the lentil soup.
- Bake:
    - Follow the pizza dough package instructions for baking. Typically, bake in a preheated oven until the crust is golden, and the cheese is melted and bubbly.
- Garnish:
    - Sprinkle chopped fresh parsley over the baked pizza.
- Serve:
    - Slice the Linsensuppe Pizza into portions and serve hot.
    - Optionally, serve with lemon wedges on the side for a bright, citrusy touch.

Enjoy the heartiness of lentil soup in a creative pizza form! Customize with additional toppings or herbs to suit your taste.

Schweinshaxe Pizza

Ingredients:

For the Schweinshaxe:

- 2 pork knuckles
- Salt and pepper to taste
- 2 tablespoons vegetable oil
- 2 cloves garlic, minced
- 1 tablespoon caraway seeds
- 1 tablespoon Dijon mustard
- 1 tablespoon honey

For the Pizza:

- 1 pizza dough (store-bought or homemade)
- 1/2 cup Bavarian sweet mustard (or Dijon mustard as a substitute)
- 1 cup shredded Emmental cheese
- 1 cup sauerkraut, drained
- Fresh parsley, chopped (for garnish)

Instructions:

For the Schweinshaxe:

Preheat Oven:
- Preheat your oven to 375°F (190°C).

Season and Roast Pork Knuckles:
- Score the skin of the pork knuckles with a sharp knife. Season with salt and pepper.
- In a roasting pan, heat vegetable oil over medium-high heat. Add the pork knuckles and sear until browned on all sides.
- In a small bowl, mix minced garlic, caraway seeds, Dijon mustard, and honey. Brush this mixture over the pork knuckles.
- Roast in the preheated oven for about 2 hours or until the pork is tender and the skin is crispy.

For the Pizza:

Preheat Oven:
- Preheat your oven according to the pizza dough package instructions.

Roll Out Pizza Dough:
- Roll out the pizza dough on a floured surface to your desired thickness.

Assemble Pizza:
- Place the rolled-out dough on a pizza stone or baking sheet.
- Spread Bavarian sweet mustard (or Dijon mustard) evenly over the dough, leaving a small border around the edges.
- Sprinkle shredded Emmental cheese evenly over the mustard.
- Distribute sauerkraut evenly over the cheese.

Add Schweinshaxe:
- Once the Schweinshaxe is roasted, remove from the oven and let it rest for a few minutes. Carve the meat from the bones and slice it.
- Place the sliced Schweinshaxe on top of the pizza.

Bake:
- Follow the pizza dough package instructions for baking. Typically, bake in a preheated oven until the crust is golden, and the toppings are heated through.

Garnish:
- Sprinkle chopped fresh parsley over the baked pizza.

Serve:
- Slice the Schweinshaxe Pizza into portions and serve hot.

Enjoy the hearty and flavorful Schweinshaxe on your pizza! Customize with additional toppings or herbs to suit your taste.

Krautwickel (Cabbage Rolls) Pizza

Ingredients:

For the Krautwickel Filling:

- 1 head of cabbage
- 1 pound ground meat (beef, pork, or a mix)
- 1 cup cooked rice
- 1 onion, finely chopped
- 2 cloves garlic, minced
- 1/2 teaspoon caraway seeds
- Salt and pepper to taste
- 1 can (14 oz) diced tomatoes

For the Pizza:

- 1 pizza dough (store-bought or homemade)
- 1 cup tomato sauce
- 1 cup shredded mozzarella cheese
- 1/2 cup sauerkraut, drained
- Fresh parsley, chopped (for garnish)

Instructions:

For the Krautwickel Filling:

- Prepare Cabbage Leaves:
    - Remove the core from the cabbage and place it in a large pot of boiling water. Boil for a few minutes until the leaves are tender and pliable. Carefully remove the leaves and set them aside.
- Prepare Filling:
    - In a bowl, combine ground meat, cooked rice, finely chopped onion, minced garlic, caraway seeds, salt, and pepper. Mix well.
- Assemble Krautwickel:
    - Place a portion of the filling in the center of each cabbage leaf. Roll the cabbage leaves around the filling, forming cabbage rolls.
- Cook Cabbage Rolls:
    - In a baking dish, arrange the cabbage rolls. Pour diced tomatoes over the top. Bake in the oven at 375°F (190°C) for about 30-40 minutes or until the cabbage is tender and the filling is cooked through.

For the Pizza:

- Preheat Oven:
  - Preheat your oven according to the pizza dough package instructions.
- Roll Out Pizza Dough:
  - Roll out the pizza dough on a floured surface to your desired thickness.
- Assemble Pizza:
  - Place the rolled-out dough on a pizza stone or baking sheet.
  - Spread tomato sauce evenly over the dough, leaving a small border around the edges.
  - Sprinkle shredded mozzarella cheese evenly over the sauce.
  - Distribute sauerkraut evenly over the cheese.
- Add Krautwickel:
  - Once the Krautwickel are cooked, remove them from the oven and let them cool slightly. Slice them into bite-sized pieces and arrange them on top of the pizza.
- Bake:
  - Follow the pizza dough package instructions for baking. Typically, bake in a preheated oven until the crust is golden, and the cheese is melted and bubbly.
- Garnish:
  - Sprinkle chopped fresh parsley over the baked pizza.
- Serve:
  - Slice the Krautwickel Pizza into portions and serve hot.

Enjoy the comforting and savory flavors of Krautwickel on your pizza! Customize with additional toppings or herbs to suit your taste.

Seasonal and Regional Varieties:

Asparagus and Ham Pizza

Ingredients:

- 1 pizza dough (store-bought or homemade)
- 1/2 cup Alfredo sauce or béchamel sauce
- 1 cup shredded mozzarella cheese
- 1 cup fresh asparagus spears, trimmed and cut into bite-sized pieces
- 1/2 cup cooked ham, diced
- Olive oil for drizzling
- Salt and pepper to taste
- Grated Parmesan cheese (optional)
- Fresh parsley, chopped (for garnish)

Instructions:

Preheat Oven:
- Preheat your oven according to the pizza dough package instructions.

Roll Out Pizza Dough:
- Roll out the pizza dough on a floured surface to your desired thickness.

Assemble Pizza:
- Place the rolled-out dough on a pizza stone or baking sheet.
- Spread Alfredo sauce or béchamel sauce evenly over the dough, leaving a small border around the edges.
- Sprinkle shredded mozzarella cheese evenly over the sauce.
- Distribute fresh asparagus pieces and diced ham evenly over the cheese.
- Drizzle a bit of olive oil over the top. Season with salt and pepper to taste.
- Optionally, sprinkle some grated Parmesan cheese for extra flavor.

Bake:
- Follow the pizza dough package instructions for baking. Typically, bake in a preheated oven until the crust is golden, and the cheese is melted and bubbly.

Garnish:
- Sprinkle chopped fresh parsley over the baked pizza.

Serve:
- Slice the Asparagus and Ham Pizza into portions and serve hot.

Enjoy the wonderful combination of asparagus and ham on your pizza! Customize with additional toppings or herbs to suit your taste.

Chanterelle Mushroom Pizza

Ingredients:

- 1 pizza dough (store-bought or homemade)
- 1 cup chanterelle mushrooms, cleaned and sliced
- 1 tablespoon olive oil
- 2 cloves garlic, minced
- 1 cup shredded mozzarella cheese
- 1/2 cup grated Parmesan cheese
- Fresh thyme leaves, for garnish
- Salt and black pepper to taste
- Optional: truffle oil for drizzling

Instructions:

Preheat Oven:
- Preheat your oven according to the pizza dough package instructions.

Prepare Chanterelle Mushrooms:
- In a skillet, heat olive oil over medium heat. Add minced garlic and sauté for about 1 minute until fragrant.
- Add the sliced chanterelle mushrooms and sauté until they are tender and any liquid released has evaporated. Season with salt and black pepper to taste. Set aside.

Roll Out Pizza Dough:
- Roll out the pizza dough on a floured surface to your desired thickness.

Assemble Pizza:
- Place the rolled-out dough on a pizza stone or baking sheet.
- Spread the sautéed chanterelle mushrooms evenly over the dough.
- Sprinkle shredded mozzarella cheese and grated Parmesan cheese over the mushrooms.

Bake:
- Follow the pizza dough package instructions for baking. Typically, bake in a preheated oven until the crust is golden, and the cheese is melted and bubbly.

Garnish:
- Once out of the oven, garnish the Chanterelle Mushroom Pizza with fresh thyme leaves.
- Optionally, drizzle truffle oil over the pizza for an extra layer of flavor.

Serve:

- Slice the Chanterelle Mushroom Pizza into portions and serve hot.

Enjoy the exquisite taste of chanterelle mushrooms on your pizza! Customize with additional toppings or herbs to suit your taste.

German Apple Strudel Pizza

Ingredients:

For the Apple Filling:

- 4 large apples (such as Granny Smith or Honeycrisp), peeled, cored, and thinly sliced
- 1/2 cup granulated sugar
- 1 teaspoon ground cinnamon
- 1/4 teaspoon ground nutmeg
- 1/4 cup raisins (optional)
- 1/4 cup chopped walnuts or almonds (optional)

For the Pizza:

- 1 pizza dough (store-bought or homemade)
- 1/4 cup unsalted butter, melted
- 1/4 cup breadcrumbs
- 1/4 cup brown sugar
- 1/2 cup vanilla custard or pastry cream
- Powdered sugar for dusting
- Vanilla ice cream (optional, for serving)

Instructions:

For the Apple Filling:

Prepare Apple Mixture:
- In a bowl, combine sliced apples, granulated sugar, ground cinnamon, ground nutmeg, raisins (if using), and chopped nuts (if using). Toss until the apples are evenly coated.

For the Pizza:

Preheat Oven:
- Preheat your oven according to the pizza dough package instructions.

Roll Out Pizza Dough:
- Roll out the pizza dough on a floured surface to your desired thickness.

Prepare Crust:
- Place the rolled-out dough on a pizza stone or baking sheet.
- Brush the dough with melted butter.

Add Breadcrumbs:

- Sprinkle breadcrumbs over the melted butter. This helps absorb excess moisture from the apples and prevents a soggy crust.

Arrange Apple Filling:
- Arrange the prepared apple mixture evenly over the crust.

Sprinkle Brown Sugar:
- Sprinkle brown sugar over the apples.

Bake:
- Follow the pizza dough package instructions for baking. Typically, bake in a preheated oven until the crust is golden, and the apples are tender.

Drizzle Custard or Pastry Cream:
- Once the pizza is out of the oven, drizzle vanilla custard or pastry cream over the apple topping.

Dust with Powdered Sugar:
- Dust the German Apple Strudel Pizza with powdered sugar.

Serve:
- Slice the pizza into portions and serve warm. Optionally, serve with a scoop of vanilla ice cream on the side.

Enjoy the delightful flavors of a German Apple Strudel in pizza form! Customize with additional toppings or glazes to suit your taste.

Cabbage and Bacon Pizza

Ingredients:

- 1 pizza dough (store-bought or homemade)
- 1 cup shredded cabbage
- 4 slices bacon, cooked and crumbled
- 1 cup shredded mozzarella cheese
- 1/4 cup grated Parmesan cheese
- 1 tablespoon olive oil
- 1 teaspoon caraway seeds (optional)
- Salt and black pepper to taste

Instructions:

Preheat Oven:
- Preheat your oven according to the pizza dough package instructions.

Roll Out Pizza Dough:
- Roll out the pizza dough on a floured surface to your desired thickness.

Prepare Pizza:
- Place the rolled-out dough on a pizza stone or baking sheet.
- Brush the surface of the dough with olive oil.

Layer Ingredients:
- Evenly spread the shredded cabbage over the pizza dough.
- Sprinkle crumbled bacon over the cabbage.
- Sprinkle shredded mozzarella and grated Parmesan cheese evenly over the toppings.
- Optionally, sprinkle caraway seeds for added flavor.

Season:
- Season the pizza with salt and black pepper to taste.

Bake:
- Follow the pizza dough package instructions for baking. Typically, bake in a preheated oven until the crust is golden, and the cheese is melted and bubbly.

Serve:
- Once out of the oven, let the pizza cool for a few minutes before slicing.
- Slice the Cabbage and Bacon Pizza into portions and serve hot.

This pizza combines the smoky flavor of bacon with the mild sweetness of cabbage for a delicious and unique taste. Feel free to customize with your favorite herbs or additional toppings to suit your preferences.

White Asparagus and Smoked Salmon Pizza

Ingredients:

- 1 pizza dough (store-bought or homemade)
- 1/2 cup crème fraîche or sour cream
- 1 cup shredded mozzarella cheese
- 1/2 pound white asparagus, trimmed and thinly sliced
- 4 ounces smoked salmon, thinly sliced
- 1 tablespoon capers, drained
- Fresh dill, chopped, for garnish
- Lemon wedges, for serving

Instructions:

Preheat Oven:
- Preheat your oven according to the pizza dough package instructions.

Roll Out Pizza Dough:
- Roll out the pizza dough on a floured surface to your desired thickness.

Prepare Pizza:
- Place the rolled-out dough on a pizza stone or baking sheet.
- Spread crème fraîche or sour cream evenly over the dough, leaving a small border around the edges.
- Sprinkle shredded mozzarella cheese evenly over the cream.

Add Toppings:
- Distribute the thinly sliced white asparagus over the cheese.
- Arrange smoked salmon slices on top of the asparagus.
- Sprinkle capers over the salmon.

Bake:
- Follow the pizza dough package instructions for baking. Typically, bake in a preheated oven until the crust is golden, and the cheese is melted and bubbly.

Garnish:
- Once out of the oven, sprinkle chopped fresh dill over the pizza.

Serve:
- Slice the White Asparagus and Smoked Salmon Pizza into portions and serve hot.
- Optionally, serve with lemon wedges on the side for a citrusy touch.

Enjoy the luxurious combination of white asparagus and smoked salmon on your pizza! Customize with additional toppings or herbs to suit your taste.

White Asparagus and Ham Hock Pizza

Ingredients:

- 1 pizza dough (store-bought or homemade)
- 1/2 cup crème fraîche or sour cream
- 1 cup shredded Gruyere cheese
- 1/2 pound white asparagus, trimmed and thinly sliced
- 1/2 cup cooked ham hock, shredded
- 1 tablespoon chopped fresh chives
- Salt and black pepper to taste

Instructions:

Preheat Oven:
- Preheat your oven according to the pizza dough package instructions.

Roll Out Pizza Dough:
- Roll out the pizza dough on a floured surface to your desired thickness.

Prepare Pizza:
- Place the rolled-out dough on a pizza stone or baking sheet.
- Spread crème fraîche or sour cream evenly over the dough, leaving a small border around the edges.
- Sprinkle shredded Gruyere cheese evenly over the cream.

Add Toppings:
- Distribute the thinly sliced white asparagus over the cheese.
- Evenly scatter the shredded ham hock over the asparagus.
- Season with salt and black pepper to taste.

Bake:
- Follow the pizza dough package instructions for baking. Typically, bake in a preheated oven until the crust is golden, and the cheese is melted and bubbly.

Garnish:
- Once out of the oven, sprinkle chopped fresh chives over the pizza.

Serve:
- Slice the White Asparagus and Ham Hock Pizza into portions and serve hot.

Enjoy the unique blend of flavors from the white asparagus and ham hock on your pizza! Customize with additional toppings or herbs to suit your taste.

Rübenkraut (Turnip Greens) and Bacon Pizza

Ingredients:

- 1 pizza dough (store-bought or homemade)
- 1/2 cup tomato sauce
- 1 cup shredded mozzarella cheese
- 1 bunch turnip greens, washed and chopped
- 4 slices bacon, cooked and crumbled
- 1/2 onion, thinly sliced
- 2 cloves garlic, minced
- Red pepper flakes (optional, for heat)
- Olive oil for drizzling
- Salt and black pepper to taste
- Grated Parmesan cheese for serving

Instructions:

Preheat Oven:
- Preheat your oven according to the pizza dough package instructions.

Roll Out Pizza Dough:
- Roll out the pizza dough on a floured surface to your desired thickness.

Prepare Pizza:
- Place the rolled-out dough on a pizza stone or baking sheet.
- Spread tomato sauce evenly over the dough, leaving a small border around the edges.
- Sprinkle shredded mozzarella cheese evenly over the sauce.

Add Toppings:
- In a skillet, sauté the thinly sliced onion and minced garlic in olive oil until softened.
- Add the chopped turnip greens to the skillet and cook until wilted. Season with salt and black pepper to taste.
- Evenly distribute the cooked turnip greens over the cheese on the pizza.
- Sprinkle crumbled bacon over the turnip greens.
- If desired, add a sprinkle of red pepper flakes for a bit of heat.

Bake:
- Follow the pizza dough package instructions for baking. Typically, bake in a preheated oven until the crust is golden, and the cheese is melted and bubbly.

Drizzle and Serve:

- Once out of the oven, drizzle a bit of olive oil over the pizza.
- Optionally, serve with grated Parmesan cheese on the side.

Slice and Enjoy:
- Slice the Rübenkraut and Bacon Pizza into portions and serve hot.

Enjoy the unique combination of turnip greens and bacon on your pizza! Customize with additional toppings or herbs to suit your taste.

Bayrischer Wurstsalat (Bavarian Sausage Salad) Pizza

Ingredients:

For the Wurstsalat:

- 1/2 pound Bavarian sausages (such as regensburger or bratwurst), thinly sliced
- 1 small red onion, thinly sliced
- 1 dill pickle, thinly sliced into strips
- 2 tablespoons white wine vinegar
- 1 tablespoon mustard
- 2 tablespoons vegetable oil
- Salt and pepper to taste
- Fresh chives, chopped, for garnish

For the Pizza:

- 1 pizza dough (store-bought or homemade)
- 1/2 cup Bavarian sweet mustard (or regular mustard as a substitute)
- 1 cup shredded Emmental cheese (or Gruyere cheese)
- 1 tablespoon caraway seeds
- Fresh parsley, chopped, for garnish

Instructions:

For the Wurstsalat:

    Prepare Wurstsalat:
- In a large bowl, combine the thinly sliced Bavarian sausages, red onion, and dill pickle strips.
- In a small bowl, whisk together white wine vinegar, mustard, vegetable oil, salt, and pepper.
- Pour the dressing over the sausage mixture and toss until well coated.
- Allow the Wurstsalat to marinate for at least 15-20 minutes.

For the Pizza:

    Preheat Oven:
- Preheat your oven according to the pizza dough package instructions.

    Roll Out Pizza Dough:
- Roll out the pizza dough on a floured surface to your desired thickness.

    Prepare Pizza:

- Place the rolled-out dough on a pizza stone or baking sheet.
- Spread Bavarian sweet mustard (or regular mustard) evenly over the dough, leaving a small border around the edges.
- Sprinkle shredded Emmental cheese evenly over the mustard.
- Distribute the marinated Wurstsalat over the cheese.

Sprinkle Caraway Seeds:
- Sprinkle caraway seeds evenly over the pizza.

Bake:
- Follow the pizza dough package instructions for baking. Typically, bake in a preheated oven until the crust is golden, and the cheese is melted and bubbly.

Garnish:
- Once out of the oven, sprinkle chopped fresh parsley over the pizza.

Serve:
- Slice the Bavarian Wurstsalat Pizza into portions and serve hot.

Enjoy the distinctive flavors of Bavarian Wurstsalat on your pizza! Customize with additional toppings or herbs to suit your taste.

Kartoffelsalat (Potato Salad) Pizza

Ingredients:

For the Potato Salad:

- 4 large potatoes, boiled and diced
- 1 small red onion, finely chopped
- 3 tablespoons vegetable oil
- 2 tablespoons white wine vinegar
- 1 tablespoon Dijon mustard
- Salt and black pepper to taste
- Fresh chives, chopped, for garnish

For the Pizza:

- 1 pizza dough (store-bought or homemade)
- 1/2 cup mayonnaise
- 1 cup shredded Gruyere or Emmental cheese
- 4 slices bacon, cooked and crumbled
- Salt and black pepper to taste
- Fresh parsley, chopped, for garnish

Instructions:

For the Potato Salad:

Prepare Potato Salad:
- In a large bowl, combine the diced boiled potatoes and finely chopped red onion.
- In a separate small bowl, whisk together vegetable oil, white wine vinegar, Dijon mustard, salt, and black pepper.
- Pour the dressing over the potatoes and toss until well coated.
- Let the Kartoffelsalat (Potato Salad) chill in the refrigerator for at least 30 minutes.

For the Pizza:

Preheat Oven:
- Preheat your oven according to the pizza dough package instructions.

Roll Out Pizza Dough:
- Roll out the pizza dough on a floured surface to your desired thickness.

Prepare Pizza:

- Place the rolled-out dough on a pizza stone or baking sheet.
- Spread mayonnaise evenly over the dough, leaving a small border around the edges.
- Sprinkle shredded Gruyere or Emmental cheese evenly over the mayonnaise.

Add Toppings:
- Distribute the chilled Kartoffelsalat over the cheese.
- Sprinkle crumbled bacon over the potato salad.
- Season with salt and black pepper to taste.

Bake:
- Follow the pizza dough package instructions for baking. Typically, bake in a preheated oven until the crust is golden, and the cheese is melted and bubbly.

Garnish:
- Once out of the oven, sprinkle chopped fresh parsley over the pizza.

Serve:
- Slice the Kartoffelsalat Pizza into portions and serve hot.

Enjoy the comforting flavors of Kartoffelsalat on your pizza! Customize with additional toppings or herbs to suit your taste.

Blaubeerpfannkuchen (Blueberry Pancake) Dessert Pizza

Ingredients:

For the Pancake Base:

- 1 cup all-purpose flour
- 2 tablespoons granulated sugar
- 1 teaspoon baking powder
- 1/2 teaspoon baking soda
- 1/4 teaspoon salt
- 3/4 cup buttermilk
- 1 large egg
- 2 tablespoons unsalted butter, melted
- 1 teaspoon vanilla extract

For the Topping:

- 1 cup fresh blueberries
- 1/4 cup brown sugar
- 1 teaspoon ground cinnamon
- 1/4 cup chopped nuts (such as almonds or pecans)
- Maple syrup for drizzling

Instructions:

Preheat Oven:
- Preheat your oven according to the pizza dough package instructions.

Prepare Pancake Base:
- In a large bowl, whisk together flour, granulated sugar, baking powder, baking soda, and salt.
- In another bowl, whisk together buttermilk, egg, melted butter, and vanilla extract.
- Pour the wet ingredients into the dry ingredients and stir until just combined. Be careful not to overmix; a few lumps are okay.

Roll Out Pancake Dough:
- Roll out the pancake dough on a floured surface to fit your pizza stone or baking sheet.

Bake Pancake Base:
- Place the rolled-out pancake dough on a pizza stone or baking sheet.

- Bake in the preheated oven until the pancake is cooked through and golden brown.

Prepare Topping:
- In a bowl, toss the fresh blueberries with brown sugar and ground cinnamon until well coated.

Assemble Dessert Pizza:
- Once the pancake base is out of the oven, spread the blueberry mixture evenly over the pancake.
- Sprinkle chopped nuts on top.

Bake Again:
- Return the dessert pizza to the oven and bake for an additional 5-7 minutes, or until the blueberries are warmed and slightly bubbly.

Drizzle with Maple Syrup:
- Drizzle the Blaubeerpfannkuchen Dessert Pizza with maple syrup just before serving.

Slice and Serve:
- Slice the dessert pizza into portions and serve warm.

Enjoy the delightful taste of Blaubeerpfannkuchen in the form of a dessert pizza! Customize with additional toppings or a dollop of whipped cream for an extra treat.

Käsespätzle and Apple Pizza

Ingredients:

For the Käsespätzle:

- 2 cups spätzle noodles (store-bought or homemade)
- 2 tablespoons butter
- 2 tablespoons all-purpose flour
- 1 1/2 cups milk
- 2 cups grated Emmental or Gruyere cheese
- Salt and black pepper to taste
- 1/2 teaspoon ground nutmeg

For the Pizza:

- 1 pizza dough (store-bought or homemade)
- 1 tablespoon olive oil
- 1 1/2 cups grated Emmental or Gruyere cheese
- 1 apple, thinly sliced
- 1/4 cup chopped walnuts
- Fresh thyme leaves, for garnish

Instructions:

For the Käsespätzle:

Cook Spätzle:
- Cook the spätzle noodles according to the package instructions or prepare homemade spätzle.

Make Cheese Sauce:
- In a large saucepan, melt butter over medium heat. Add flour and stir to form a roux.
- Gradually whisk in the milk, ensuring no lumps form.
- Stir in grated cheese until melted and smooth.
- Season with salt, black pepper, and ground nutmeg.
- Add cooked spätzle to the cheese sauce, tossing to coat. Set aside.

For the Pizza:

Preheat Oven:
- Preheat your oven according to the pizza dough package instructions.

Roll Out Pizza Dough:
- Roll out the pizza dough on a floured surface to your desired thickness.

Prepare Pizza:
- Place the rolled-out dough on a pizza stone or baking sheet.
- Brush the surface of the dough with olive oil.

Layer Ingredients:
- Evenly spread the prepared Käsespätzle over the pizza dough.
- Sprinkle additional grated Emmental or Gruyere cheese over the spätzle.
- Arrange thin apple slices on top.
- Scatter chopped walnuts over the pizza.

Bake:
- Follow the pizza dough package instructions for baking. Typically, bake in a preheated oven until the crust is golden, and the cheese is melted and bubbly.

Garnish:
- Once out of the oven, garnish the pizza with fresh thyme leaves.

Slice and Serve:
- Slice the Käsespätzle and Apple Pizza into portions and serve hot.

Enjoy the delicious combination of cheesy spätzle and sweet apples on your pizza! Customize with additional toppings or herbs to suit your taste.

Brezenknödel (Pretzel Dumpling) Pizza

Ingredients:

For the Pretzel Dumplings:

- 4 Brezenknödel (pretzel dumplings), sliced
- 2 tablespoons butter
- 1 onion, finely chopped
- 2 cloves garlic, minced
- Salt and black pepper to taste
- Chopped fresh parsley for garnish

For the Pizza:

- 1 pizza dough (store-bought or homemade)
- 1/2 cup Dijon mustard
- 1 1/2 cups shredded Swiss cheese
- 1 cup sauerkraut, drained
- 4 slices cooked and crumbled bacon
- Chopped fresh chives for garnish

Instructions:

For the Pretzel Dumplings:

Prepare Pretzel Dumplings:
- Slice the Brezenknödel into rounds.
- In a skillet, melt butter over medium heat. Add finely chopped onion and minced garlic. Sauté until the onion is translucent.
- Add the sliced pretzel dumplings to the skillet and sauté until they are golden brown.
- Season with salt and black pepper to taste.
- Garnish with chopped fresh parsley and set aside.

For the Pizza:

Preheat Oven:
- Preheat your oven according to the pizza dough package instructions.

Roll Out Pizza Dough:
- Roll out the pizza dough on a floured surface to your desired thickness.

Prepare Pizza:

- Place the rolled-out dough on a pizza stone or baking sheet.
- Spread Dijon mustard evenly over the dough, leaving a small border around the edges.
- Sprinkle shredded Swiss cheese evenly over the mustard.

Add Toppings:
- Arrange the sautéed pretzel dumplings on top of the cheese.
- Distribute drained sauerkraut over the pizza.
- Sprinkle crumbled bacon over the sauerkraut.

Bake:
- Follow the pizza dough package instructions for baking. Typically, bake in a preheated oven until the crust is golden, and the cheese is melted and bubbly.

Garnish:
- Once out of the oven, garnish the pizza with chopped fresh chives.

Slice and Serve:
- Slice the Brezenknödel Pizza into portions and serve hot.

Enjoy the distinctive flavors of pretzel dumplings on your pizza! Customize with additional toppings or herbs to suit your taste.

Pflaumenkuchen (Plum Cake) Dessert Pizza

Ingredients:

For the Dough:

- 1 pizza dough (store-bought or homemade)

For the Topping:

- 4-5 ripe plums, pitted and sliced
- 1/4 cup sugar
- 1 teaspoon ground cinnamon
- 1/4 cup sliced almonds

For the Crumb Topping:

- 1/2 cup all-purpose flour
- 1/4 cup sugar
- 1/4 cup cold unsalted butter, cut into small pieces

For Garnish:

- Powdered sugar for dusting
- Vanilla ice cream (optional, for serving)

Instructions:

Preheat Oven:
- Preheat your oven according to the pizza dough package instructions.

Roll Out Pizza Dough:
- Roll out the pizza dough on a floured surface to your desired thickness.

Prepare Crumb Topping:
- In a small bowl, combine flour, sugar, and cold butter pieces. Use your fingers to rub the butter into the dry ingredients until crumbs form. Set aside.

Assemble Pizza:
- Place the rolled-out dough on a pizza stone or baking sheet.
- Arrange the plum slices evenly over the dough.
- Sprinkle sugar and ground cinnamon over the plums.
- Evenly distribute the crumb topping over the plums.
- Sprinkle sliced almonds over the crumb topping.

Bake:
- Follow the pizza dough package instructions for baking. Typically, bake in a preheated oven until the crust is golden, and the plums are tender.

Garnish:
- Once out of the oven, let the pizza cool for a few minutes.
- Dust the Pflaumenkuchen Dessert Pizza with powdered sugar.

Serve:
- Slice the dessert pizza into portions and serve warm.
- Optionally, serve with a scoop of vanilla ice cream on the side.

Enjoy the delicious combination of plum cake flavors on your dessert pizza! Customize with additional toppings or a drizzle of caramel for an extra treat.

Weißwurst (White Sausage) and Mustard Pizza

Ingredients:

For the Pizza:

- 1 pizza dough (store-bought or homemade)
- 1/2 cup yellow mustard
- 1 1/2 cups shredded Bavarian white cheese (such as Emmental or Gruyere)
- 6 Weißwurst (white sausages), cooked and sliced
- 1 small red onion, thinly sliced
- Fresh chives, chopped, for garnish

Instructions:

   Preheat Oven:
- Preheat your oven according to the pizza dough package instructions.

   Roll Out Pizza Dough:
- Roll out the pizza dough on a floured surface to your desired thickness.

   Prepare Pizza:
- Place the rolled-out dough on a pizza stone or baking sheet.
- Spread yellow mustard evenly over the dough, leaving a small border around the edges.
- Sprinkle shredded Bavarian white cheese evenly over the mustard.

   Add Toppings:
- Distribute the sliced Weißwurst (white sausages) over the cheese.
- Scatter thinly sliced red onions over the sausages.

   Bake:
- Follow the pizza dough package instructions for baking. Typically, bake in a preheated oven until the crust is golden, and the cheese is melted and bubbly.

   Garnish:
- Once out of the oven, sprinkle chopped fresh chives over the pizza.

   Slice and Serve:
- Slice the Weißwurst and Mustard Pizza into portions and serve hot.

Enjoy the unique combination of white sausage and mustard on your pizza! Customize with additional toppings or herbs to suit your taste.

Grünkohl (Kale) and Smoked Pork Pizza

Ingredients:

For the Pizza:

- 1 pizza dough (store-bought or homemade)
- 1/2 cup tomato sauce
- 1 1/2 cups shredded mozzarella cheese
- 1 cup chopped kale, stems removed
- 1/2 cup smoked pork, diced
- 1 small red onion, thinly sliced
- 2 cloves garlic, minced
- Olive oil for drizzling
- Salt and black pepper to taste
- Grated Parmesan cheese for serving

Instructions:

Preheat Oven:
- Preheat your oven according to the pizza dough package instructions.

Roll Out Pizza Dough:
- Roll out the pizza dough on a floured surface to your desired thickness.

Prepare Pizza:
- Place the rolled-out dough on a pizza stone or baking sheet.
- Spread tomato sauce evenly over the dough, leaving a small border around the edges.
- Sprinkle shredded mozzarella cheese evenly over the sauce.

Add Toppings:
- Distribute chopped kale, diced smoked pork, thinly sliced red onions, and minced garlic over the cheese.
- Season with salt and black pepper to taste.

Drizzle with Olive Oil:
- Drizzle a bit of olive oil over the pizza.

Bake:
- Follow the pizza dough package instructions for baking. Typically, bake in a preheated oven until the crust is golden, and the cheese is melted and bubbly.

Serve:
- Once out of the oven, let the pizza cool for a few minutes before slicing.

- Optionally, serve with grated Parmesan cheese on the side.

Slice and Enjoy:
- Slice the Grünkohl and Smoked Pork Pizza into portions and serve hot.

Enjoy the rich and savory flavors of kale and smoked pork on your pizza! Customize with additional toppings or herbs to suit your taste.

Fusion and Creative Varieties:

Currywurst Pizza

Ingredients:

For the Pizza:
- 1 pizza dough (store-bought or homemade)
- 1/2 cup tomato sauce
- 1 1/2 cups shredded mozzarella cheese
- 1 cup cooked and sliced bratwurst or other German sausages
- 1/2 cup curry ketchup (mix regular ketchup with curry powder to taste)
- 1 small red onion, thinly sliced
- 1 tablespoon curry powder
- Fresh parsley, chopped, for garnish

Instructions:

Preheat Oven:
- Preheat your oven according to the pizza dough package instructions.

Roll Out Pizza Dough:
- Roll out the pizza dough on a floured surface to your desired thickness.

Prepare Pizza:
- Place the rolled-out dough on a pizza stone or baking sheet.
- Spread tomato sauce evenly over the dough, leaving a small border around the edges.
- Sprinkle shredded mozzarella cheese evenly over the sauce.

Add Toppings:
- Distribute the cooked and sliced bratwurst over the cheese.
- Drizzle curry ketchup over the bratwurst and cheese.
- Scatter thinly sliced red onions over the pizza.
- Sprinkle curry powder evenly over the toppings.

Bake:
- Follow the pizza dough package instructions for baking. Typically, bake in a preheated oven until the crust is golden, and the cheese is melted and bubbly.

Garnish:
- Once out of the oven, garnish the pizza with chopped fresh parsley.

Slice and Serve:

- Slice the Currywurst Pizza into portions and serve hot.

Enjoy the bold and savory flavors of currywurst on your pizza! Customize with additional toppings or a drizzle of extra curry ketchup for an extra kick.

German Beer Cheese and Brat Pizza

Ingredients:

For the Pizza:

- 1 pizza dough (store-bought or homemade)
- 1/2 cup German beer cheese spread
- 1 1/2 cups shredded Swiss cheese
- 4 bratwurst sausages, cooked and sliced
- 1 small red onion, thinly sliced
- 1 tablespoon Dijon mustard
- Fresh parsley, chopped, for garnish

Instructions:

Preheat Oven:
- Preheat your oven according to the pizza dough package instructions.

Roll Out Pizza Dough:
- Roll out the pizza dough on a floured surface to your desired thickness.

Prepare Pizza:
- Place the rolled-out dough on a pizza stone or baking sheet.
- Spread German beer cheese evenly over the dough, leaving a small border around the edges.
- Sprinkle shredded Swiss cheese evenly over the beer cheese.

Add Toppings:
- Distribute the cooked and sliced bratwurst over the cheese.
- Scatter thinly sliced red onions over the pizza.
- Drizzle Dijon mustard over the toppings.

Bake:
- Follow the pizza dough package instructions for baking. Typically, bake in a preheated oven until the crust is golden, and the cheese is melted and bubbly.

Garnish:
- Once out of the oven, garnish the pizza with chopped fresh parsley.

Slice and Serve:
- Slice the German Beer Cheese and Brat Pizza into portions and serve hot.

Enjoy the rich and savory flavors of German beer cheese and bratwurst on your pizza!

Customize with additional toppings or herbs to suit your taste.

Black Forest Cherry Chocolate Pizza

Ingredients:

For the Pizza Dough:

- 1 pizza dough (store-bought or homemade)

For the Toppings:

- 1 cup chocolate spread or Nutella
- 1 cup canned or jarred dark cherries, drained
- 1/2 cup dark chocolate shavings or curls
- 1/4 cup sliced almonds, toasted
- Powdered sugar for dusting
- Whipped cream for serving (optional)

Instructions:

Preheat Oven:
- Preheat your oven according to the pizza dough package instructions.

Roll Out Pizza Dough:
- Roll out the pizza dough on a floured surface to your desired thickness.

Prepare Pizza:
- Place the rolled-out dough on a pizza stone or baking sheet.
- Spread chocolate spread or Nutella evenly over the dough, leaving a small border around the edges.

Add Toppings:
- Distribute drained dark cherries over the chocolate spread.
- Sprinkle dark chocolate shavings or curls over the cherries.
- Evenly scatter toasted sliced almonds on top.

Bake:
- Follow the pizza dough package instructions for baking. Typically, bake in a preheated oven until the crust is golden.

Garnish:
- Once out of the oven, let the pizza cool for a few minutes.
- Dust the Black Forest Cherry Chocolate Pizza with powdered sugar.

Serve:
- Optionally, serve with a dollop of whipped cream on top.

Slice and Enjoy:

- Slice the dessert pizza into portions and serve warm.

Enjoy the indulgent and decadent flavors of Black Forest cake on your pizza! Customize with additional toppings or add a scoop of vanilla ice cream for an extra treat.

Pretzel Crust Schnitzel Pizza

Ingredients:

For the Pretzel Crust:

- 1 1/2 cups warm water
- 1 tablespoon sugar
- 2 teaspoons active dry yeast
- 4 cups all-purpose flour
- 1 teaspoon salt
- 2 tablespoons baking soda
- Coarse salt for sprinkling

For the Pizza Toppings:

- 1 cup Dijon mustard
- 1 1/2 cups shredded Swiss cheese
- 4 pork schnitzel, cooked and sliced
- 1 small red onion, thinly sliced
- Fresh parsley, chopped, for garnish

Instructions:

For the Pretzel Crust:

Prepare Pretzel Dough:
- In a bowl, combine warm water and sugar. Sprinkle yeast over the water and let it sit for about 5 minutes, or until foamy.
- In a large mixing bowl, combine flour and salt. Pour in the yeast mixture and stir to form a dough.
- Knead the dough on a floured surface until smooth. Place it in a greased bowl, cover, and let it rise for about 1 hour, or until doubled in size.

Shape Pretzel Crust:
- Preheat the oven according to the pizza dough package instructions.
- Punch down the risen dough and divide it into two portions.
- Roll out each portion into a circle on a floured surface, forming your pizza crusts.

Boil Pretzel Crust:
- In a large pot, bring water to a boil. Add baking soda.
- Gently place each pizza crust into the boiling water for about 30 seconds on each side. Remove and let excess water drain off.

Bake Pretzel Crust:

- Place the boiled pizza crusts on a baking sheet or pizza stone.
- Sprinkle with coarse salt.
- Bake according to the pizza dough package instructions, or until the crust is golden brown.

For the Pizza Toppings:

Prepare Pizza:
- Preheat your oven according to the pizza dough package instructions.

Spread Dijon Mustard:
- Spread Dijon mustard evenly over the pretzel crusts, leaving a small border around the edges.

Add Cheese and Toppings:
- Sprinkle shredded Swiss cheese over the mustard.
- Distribute the cooked and sliced pork schnitzel over the cheese.
- Scatter thinly sliced red onions on top.

Bake:
- Follow the pizza dough package instructions for baking. Typically, bake until the cheese is melted and bubbly.

Garnish:
- Once out of the oven, sprinkle chopped fresh parsley over the pizza.

Slice and Serve:
- Slice the Pretzel Crust Schnitzel Pizza into portions and serve hot.

Enjoy the delicious combination of pretzel crust and schnitzel on your pizza! Customize with additional toppings or herbs to suit your taste.

Rote Grütze Dessert Pizza

Ingredients:

For the Pizza Dough:

- 1 pizza dough (store-bought or homemade)

For the Rote Grütze Topping:

- 2 cups mixed berries (strawberries, raspberries, blackberries, red currants)
- 1/2 cup granulated sugar
- 2 tablespoons cornstarch
- 1 tablespoon lemon juice
- 1/2 teaspoon vanilla extract

For the Cream Cheese Drizzle:

- 4 oz cream cheese, softened
- 1/4 cup powdered sugar
- 2 tablespoons milk
- 1/2 teaspoon vanilla extract

Additional Garnish:

- Fresh mint leaves for garnish
- Powdered sugar for dusting

Instructions:

For the Pizza Dough:

Preheat Oven:
- Preheat your oven according to the pizza dough package instructions.

Roll Out Pizza Dough:
- Roll out the pizza dough on a floured surface to your desired thickness.

Bake Pizza Dough:
- Place the rolled-out dough on a pizza stone or baking sheet.
- Follow the pizza dough package instructions for baking. Typically, bake until the crust is golden brown.

For the Rote Grütze Topping:

Prepare Berry Compote:
- In a saucepan, combine mixed berries, granulated sugar, cornstarch, lemon juice, and vanilla extract.
- Cook over medium heat, stirring constantly until the berries break down and the mixture thickens into a compote. This typically takes about 10-15 minutes.
- Remove from heat and let it cool.

For the Cream Cheese Drizzle:

Make Cream Cheese Drizzle:
- In a bowl, whisk together softened cream cheese, powdered sugar, milk, and vanilla extract until smooth.

Assembling the Pizza:

Assemble Pizza:
- Once the pizza crust is baked and cooled, spread the Rote Grütze berry compote over the crust.

Drizzle with Cream Cheese:
- Drizzle the cream cheese mixture over the berry compote.

Garnish:
- Garnish the Rote Grütze Dessert Pizza with fresh mint leaves and a dusting of powdered sugar.

Slice and Serve:
- Slice the dessert pizza into portions and serve.

Enjoy the refreshing and fruity flavors of Rote Grütze on your pizza! Customize with additional berries or a scoop of vanilla ice cream for an extra treat.

Käsespätzle Pizza

Ingredients:

For the Pizza Dough:

- 1 pizza dough (store-bought or homemade)

For the Käsespätzle Topping:

- 2 cups cooked spaetzle noodles (store-bought or homemade)
- 2 tablespoons butter
- 1 small onion, finely chopped
- 2 cups shredded Emmental or Gruyere cheese
- Salt and black pepper to taste
- Nutmeg, a pinch (optional)
- Chopped fresh chives or parsley for garnish

Instructions:

For the Pizza Dough:

Preheat Oven:
- Preheat your oven according to the pizza dough package instructions.

Roll Out Pizza Dough:
- Roll out the pizza dough on a floured surface to your desired thickness.

Bake Pizza Dough:
- Place the rolled-out dough on a pizza stone or baking sheet.
- Follow the pizza dough package instructions for baking. Typically, bake until the crust is golden brown.

For the Käsespätzle Topping:

Prepare Käsespätzle:
- In a large skillet, melt butter over medium heat. Add finely chopped onions and sauté until translucent.
- Add the cooked spaetzle noodles to the skillet and toss to coat with the butter and onions.
- Sprinkle shredded cheese over the spaetzle and continue to cook, stirring frequently, until the cheese is melted and bubbly.
- Season with salt, black pepper, and a pinch of nutmeg if desired.

- Remove from heat.

Assembling the Pizza:

    Assemble Pizza:
- Once the pizza crust is baked and cooled, spread the Käsespätzle mixture over the crust.

    Garnish:
- Garnish the Käsespätzle Pizza with chopped fresh chives or parsley.

    Slice and Serve:
- Slice the pizza into portions and serve warm.

Enjoy the comforting and cheesy goodness of Käsespätzle on your pizza! Customize with additional toppings like caramelized onions or crispy bacon if desired.

Apfelstrudel Pizza

Ingredients:

For the Pizza Dough:

- 1 pizza dough (store-bought or homemade)

For the Apfelstrudel Topping:

- 2 large apples (such as Granny Smith), peeled, cored, and thinly sliced
- 1/4 cup unsalted butter
- 1/2 cup brown sugar
- 1 teaspoon ground cinnamon
- 1/4 teaspoon ground nutmeg
- 1/2 cup raisins (optional)
- 1/2 cup chopped walnuts or almonds
- 1 tablespoon lemon juice

For the Streusel Topping:

- 1/2 cup all-purpose flour
- 1/4 cup granulated sugar
- 1/4 cup unsalted butter, cold and diced

For Garnish:

- Powdered sugar for dusting
- Vanilla ice cream or whipped cream (optional)

Instructions:

For the Pizza Dough:

Preheat Oven:
- Preheat your oven according to the pizza dough package instructions.

Roll Out Pizza Dough:
- Roll out the pizza dough on a floured surface to your desired thickness.

Bake Pizza Dough:
- Place the rolled-out dough on a pizza stone or baking sheet.
- Follow the pizza dough package instructions for baking. Typically, bake until the crust is golden brown.

For the Apfelstrudel Topping:

Prepare Apfelstrudel Mixture:
- In a large skillet, melt butter over medium heat.
- Add sliced apples, brown sugar, ground cinnamon, ground nutmeg, raisins (if using), chopped nuts, and lemon juice.
- Cook, stirring occasionally, until the apples are tender and the sugar has caramelized. This typically takes about 10-15 minutes.
- Remove from heat and let it cool.

For the Streusel Topping:

Make Streusel Topping:
- In a bowl, combine flour, granulated sugar, and cold diced butter.
- Use your fingers to rub the butter into the dry ingredients until crumbs form.

Assembling the Pizza:

Assemble Pizza:
- Once the pizza crust is baked and cooled, spread the cooked Apfelstrudel mixture over the crust.

Add Streusel Topping:
- Sprinkle the streusel topping over the Apfelstrudel mixture.

Bake:
- Return the pizza to the oven and bake for an additional 10-15 minutes, or until the streusel is golden brown.

Garnish:
- Once out of the oven, let the pizza cool for a few minutes.
- Dust the Apfelstrudel Pizza with powdered sugar.

Serve:
- Optionally, serve with a scoop of vanilla ice cream or whipped cream on the side.

Slice and Enjoy:
- Slice the dessert pizza into portions and serve warm.

Enjoy the delightful taste of Apfelstrudel on your pizza! Customize with additional toppings or drizzle with caramel for an extra treat.

Döner Kebab Pizza

Ingredients:

For the Pizza Dough:

- 1 pizza dough (store-bought or homemade)

For the Döner Kebab Topping:

- 1 cup thinly sliced cooked döner kebab meat (lamb, chicken, or beef)
- 1/2 cup diced tomatoes
- 1/2 cup diced cucumbers
- 1/4 cup thinly sliced red onions
- 1/4 cup chopped fresh parsley

For the Yogurt Sauce:

- 1 cup Greek yogurt
- 1 clove garlic, minced
- 1 tablespoon lemon juice
- 1 tablespoon olive oil
- Salt and black pepper to taste

For Garnish:

- Sliced lemons
- Hot sauce or tahini sauce (optional)

Instructions:

For the Pizza Dough:

Preheat Oven:
- Preheat your oven according to the pizza dough package instructions.

Roll Out Pizza Dough:
- Roll out the pizza dough on a floured surface to your desired thickness.

Bake Pizza Dough:
- Place the rolled-out dough on a pizza stone or baking sheet.
- Follow the pizza dough package instructions for baking. Typically, bake until the crust is golden brown.

For the Döner Kebab Topping:

Prepare Döner Kebab Toppings:
- In a skillet over medium heat, warm the sliced döner kebab meat until heated through.

Assemble Pizza:
- Once the pizza crust is baked and cooled, spread the cooked döner kebab meat over the crust.

Add Fresh Toppings:
- Sprinkle diced tomatoes, diced cucumbers, thinly sliced red onions, and chopped fresh parsley over the döner kebab meat.

For the Yogurt Sauce:

Make Yogurt Sauce:
- In a bowl, mix together Greek yogurt, minced garlic, lemon juice, olive oil, salt, and black pepper.

Drizzle Yogurt Sauce:
- Drizzle the yogurt sauce over the pizza toppings.

Garnish:
- Garnish the Döner Kebab Pizza with sliced lemons.
- Optionally, drizzle with hot sauce or tahini sauce for extra flavor.

Slice and Serve:
- Slice the pizza into portions and serve immediately.

Enjoy the delightful taste of Döner Kebab on your pizza! Customize with additional toppings or sauces to suit your taste.

Sauerbraten Pizza

Ingredients:

For the Pizza Dough:

- 1 pizza dough (store-bought or homemade)

For the Sauerbraten Topping:

- 1 cup cooked and shredded Sauerbraten meat
- 1 cup red cabbage, thinly sliced
- 1/2 cup pickled gherkins, sliced
- 1/4 cup red onions, thinly sliced
- 1 cup shredded Swiss cheese or Gouda

For the Gravy Drizzle:

- 1/2 cup Sauerbraten gravy (strained)

Additional Garnish:

- Fresh parsley, chopped
- Mustard for serving (optional)

Instructions:

For the Pizza Dough:

    Preheat Oven:
- Preheat your oven according to the pizza dough package instructions.

    Roll Out Pizza Dough:
- Roll out the pizza dough on a floured surface to your desired thickness.

    Bake Pizza Dough:
- Place the rolled-out dough on a pizza stone or baking sheet.
- Follow the pizza dough package instructions for baking. Typically, bake until the crust is golden brown.

For the Sauerbraten Topping:

    Prepare Sauerbraten Toppings:
- In a skillet over medium heat, warm the shredded Sauerbraten meat until heated through.

    Assemble Pizza:

- Once the pizza crust is baked and cooled, spread the cooked Sauerbraten meat over the crust.

Add Fresh Toppings:
- Sprinkle thinly sliced red cabbage, sliced pickled gherkins, thinly sliced red onions, and shredded Swiss cheese or Gouda over the Sauerbraten meat.

For the Gravy Drizzle:

Warm Sauerbraten Gravy:
- In a small saucepan, warm the Sauerbraten gravy over low heat.

Drizzle Gravy:
- Drizzle the warm Sauerbraten gravy over the pizza toppings.

Additional Garnish:

Garnish:
- Sprinkle chopped fresh parsley over the pizza.

Serve with Mustard:
- Optionally, serve the Sauerbraten Pizza with a side of mustard for dipping.

Slice and Serve:
- Slice the pizza into portions and serve hot.

Enjoy the bold and tangy flavors of Sauerbraten on your pizza! Customize with additional toppings or adjust the amount of gravy according to your preference.

German Curry Pizza

Ingredients:

For the Pizza Dough:

- 1 pizza dough (store-bought or homemade)

For the Currywurst Topping:

- 1 cup cooked and sliced bratwurst or German sausage
- 1/2 cup currywurst sauce (a mix of ketchup and curry powder to taste)
- 1 cup shredded mozzarella cheese
- 1/4 cup red onions, thinly sliced
- 1/4 cup bell peppers, thinly sliced
- 1/4 cup corn kernels
- Fresh cilantro, chopped, for garnish

Instructions:

For the Pizza Dough:

Preheat Oven:
- Preheat your oven according to the pizza dough package instructions.

Roll Out Pizza Dough:
- Roll out the pizza dough on a floured surface to your desired thickness.

Bake Pizza Dough:
- Place the rolled-out dough on a pizza stone or baking sheet.
- Follow the pizza dough package instructions for baking. Typically, bake until the crust is golden brown.

For the Currywurst Topping:

Prepare Currywurst Toppings:
- In a skillet over medium heat, warm the sliced bratwurst or German sausage until heated through.

Assemble Pizza:
- Once the pizza crust is baked and cooled, spread the currywurst sauce over the crust.

Add Fresh Toppings:
- Sprinkle shredded mozzarella cheese over the currywurst sauce.
- Distribute the cooked and sliced bratwurst or German sausage over the cheese.

- Scatter thinly sliced red onions, sliced bell peppers, and corn kernels over the pizza.

Additional Garnish:

Garnish:
- Sprinkle chopped fresh cilantro over the pizza.

Serve:
- Once out of the oven, let the pizza cool for a few minutes.
- Slice the Currywurst Pizza into portions and serve hot.

Enjoy the spicy and savory flavors of currywurst on your pizza! Customize with additional toppings or adjust the currywurst sauce to your preferred level of spiciness.

Vegetarian and Vegan Options:

German Potato Salad Pizza

Ingredients:

For the Pizza Dough:

- 1 pizza dough (store-bought or homemade)

For the German Potato Salad Topping:

- 3 medium-sized potatoes, boiled and sliced
- 1/4 cup vegetable broth
- 2 tablespoons apple cider vinegar
- 1 tablespoon Dijon mustard
- 1 tablespoon olive oil
- 1 small red onion, thinly sliced
- 2 tablespoons chopped fresh parsley
- Salt and black pepper to taste

For Vegan Cheese Sauce:

- 1 cup peeled and diced potatoes
- 1/4 cup peeled and diced carrots
- 1/4 cup nutritional yeast
- 2 tablespoons olive oil
- 1 tablespoon lemon juice
- 1/2 teaspoon garlic powder
- 1/2 teaspoon onion powder
- Salt and black pepper to taste

Additional Garnish:

- Chopped chives or green onions
- Vegan bacon bits (optional)

Instructions:

For the Pizza Dough:

Preheat Oven:
- Preheat your oven according to the pizza dough package instructions.

Roll Out Pizza Dough:
- Roll out the pizza dough on a floured surface to your desired thickness.

Bake Pizza Dough:
- Place the rolled-out dough on a pizza stone or baking sheet.
- Follow the pizza dough package instructions for baking. Typically, bake until the crust is golden brown.

For the German Potato Salad Topping:

Prepare Potato Salad Toppings:
- In a bowl, mix together boiled and sliced potatoes, vegetable broth, apple cider vinegar, Dijon mustard, olive oil, thinly sliced red onions, and chopped fresh parsley.
- Season with salt and black pepper to taste. Toss until the potatoes are well coated.

For Vegan Cheese Sauce:

Make Vegan Cheese Sauce:
- In a pot, boil the diced potatoes and carrots until tender. Drain.

Blend Cheese Sauce:
- In a blender, combine the boiled potatoes and carrots with nutritional yeast, olive oil, lemon juice, garlic powder, onion powder, salt, and black pepper. Blend until smooth.

Assembling the Pizza:

Assemble Pizza:
- Once the pizza crust is baked and cooled, spread the German Potato Salad mixture over the crust.

Drizzle with Vegan Cheese Sauce:
- Drizzle the vegan cheese sauce over the potato salad.

Bake:
- Return the pizza to the oven and bake for an additional 5-7 minutes, or until toppings are heated through.

Additional Garnish:

Garnish:
- Sprinkle chopped chives or green onions and vegan bacon bits (if using) over the pizza.

Serve:

- Slice the Vegetarian and Vegan German Potato Salad Pizza into portions and serve hot.

Enjoy this unique and flavorful pizza with all the delicious elements of German potato salad! Adjust toppings and flavors to your liking.

Vegan Sauerkraut and Tempeh Pizza

Ingredients:

For the Pizza Dough:

- 1 pizza dough (store-bought or homemade)

For the Sauerkraut and Tempeh Topping:

- 1 cup sauerkraut, drained
- 1 package (about 8 oz) tempeh, crumbled
- 1 tablespoon olive oil
- 2 cloves garlic, minced
- 1 teaspoon caraway seeds
- Salt and black pepper to taste

For Vegan Thousand Island Dressing:

- 1/2 cup vegan mayonnaise
- 2 tablespoons ketchup
- 1 tablespoon sweet pickle relish
- 1 teaspoon white vinegar
- Salt and black pepper to taste

Additional Toppings:

- 1 cup shredded vegan cheese (cheddar or mozzarella)
- 1/4 cup sliced green onions
- Fresh dill for garnish

Instructions:

For the Pizza Dough:

Preheat Oven:
- Preheat your oven according to the pizza dough package instructions.

Roll Out Pizza Dough:
- Roll out the pizza dough on a floured surface to your desired thickness.

Bake Pizza Dough:
- Place the rolled-out dough on a pizza stone or baking sheet.

- Follow the pizza dough package instructions for baking. Typically, bake until the crust is golden brown.

For the Sauerkraut and Tempeh Topping:

Prepare Sauerkraut and Tempeh:
- In a skillet, heat olive oil over medium heat. Add minced garlic and crumbled tempeh. Sauté until tempeh is golden brown.

Add Seasoning:
- Sprinkle caraway seeds over the tempeh and mix well. Season with salt and black pepper to taste.

Assemble Pizza:
- Once the pizza crust is baked and cooled, spread the sauerkraut over the crust.

Add Tempeh Mixture:
- Spread the sautéed tempeh mixture evenly over the sauerkraut.

For Vegan Thousand Island Dressing:

Make Vegan Thousand Island Dressing:
- In a bowl, whisk together vegan mayonnaise, ketchup, sweet pickle relish, white vinegar, salt, and black pepper.

Assembling the Pizza:

Drizzle with Dressing:
- Drizzle the Vegan Thousand Island dressing over the sauerkraut and tempeh.

Add Vegan Cheese and Toppings:
- Sprinkle shredded vegan cheese over the pizza.
- Add sliced green onions on top.

Bake:
- Return the pizza to the oven and bake for an additional 8-10 minutes, or until the vegan cheese is melted and bubbly.

Additional Garnish:

Garnish:
- Garnish the Vegan Sauerkraut and Tempeh Pizza with fresh dill.

Slice and Serve:
- Slice the pizza into portions and serve hot.

Enjoy the tangy and savory flavors of sauerkraut and tempeh on your vegan pizza! Adjust toppings and seasonings according to your taste.

Spargel (White Asparagus) and Hollandaise Pizza

Ingredients:

For the Pizza Dough:

- 1 pizza dough (store-bought or homemade)

For the Spargel and Hollandaise Topping:

- 1 bunch of white asparagus, trimmed and peeled
- 2 tablespoons olive oil
- Salt and black pepper to taste
- 1 cup vegan hollandaise sauce (recipe below)
- 1 cup vegan cheese (mozzarella or a blend), shredded

For Vegan Hollandaise Sauce:

- 1 cup unsweetened plant-based milk (e.g., soy or almond)
- 1/2 cup refined coconut oil, melted
- 2 tablespoons nutritional yeast
- 1 tablespoon cornstarch
- 1 tablespoon lemon juice
- 1/2 teaspoon turmeric (for color)
- Salt and cayenne pepper to taste

Additional Garnish:

- Fresh chives, chopped
- Lemon wedges for serving

Instructions:

For the Pizza Dough:

    Preheat Oven:
- Preheat your oven according to the pizza dough package instructions.

    Roll Out Pizza Dough:
- Roll out the pizza dough on a floured surface to your desired thickness.

    Bake Pizza Dough:
- Place the rolled-out dough on a pizza stone or baking sheet.
- Follow the pizza dough package instructions for baking. Typically, bake until the crust is golden brown.

For the Spargel and Hollandaise Topping:

Prepare Spargel:
- Preheat the oven to 400°F (200°C).
- Toss peeled white asparagus in olive oil, salt, and black pepper.
- Roast in the preheated oven for about 15-20 minutes, or until tender.

Make Vegan Hollandaise Sauce:
- In a blender, combine plant-based milk, melted coconut oil, nutritional yeast, cornstarch, lemon juice, turmeric, salt, and cayenne pepper.
- Blend until smooth.

Assembling the Pizza:

Assemble Pizza:
- Once the pizza crust is baked and cooled, spread the vegan hollandaise sauce over the crust.

Add Roasted Spargel:
- Place the roasted white asparagus spears evenly over the hollandaise sauce.

Sprinkle Vegan Cheese:
- Sprinkle shredded vegan cheese over the pizza.

Bake:
- Return the pizza to the oven and bake for an additional 8-10 minutes, or until the vegan cheese is melted and bubbly.

Additional Garnish:

Garnish:
- Garnish the Spargel and Hollandaise Pizza with chopped fresh chives.

Serve:
- Slice the pizza into portions and serve hot with lemon wedges on the side.

Enjoy the unique combination of white asparagus and hollandaise sauce on your pizza! Adjust toppings and seasonings according to your taste.

German-style Zucchini and Leek Pizza

Ingredients:

For the Pizza Dough:

- 1 pizza dough (store-bought or homemade)

For the Zucchini and Leek Topping:

- 2 medium zucchinis, thinly sliced
- 1 leek, washed and thinly sliced
- 2 tablespoons olive oil
- Salt and black pepper to taste
- 1 teaspoon dried thyme
- 1 cup shredded Emmental or Gruyere cheese

For the Crème Fraîche Drizzle:

- 1/2 cup vegan crème fraîche (store-bought or homemade)
- 1 clove garlic, minced
- 1 tablespoon fresh lemon juice
- Salt and black pepper to taste

Additional Garnish:

- Fresh parsley, chopped
- Lemon zest

Instructions:

For the Pizza Dough:

Preheat Oven:
- Preheat your oven according to the pizza dough package instructions.

Roll Out Pizza Dough:
- Roll out the pizza dough on a floured surface to your desired thickness.

Bake Pizza Dough:
- Place the rolled-out dough on a pizza stone or baking sheet.
- Follow the pizza dough package instructions for baking. Typically, bake until the crust is golden brown.

For the Zucchini and Leek Topping:

Prepare Zucchini and Leek:
- In a skillet, heat olive oil over medium heat.
- Add thinly sliced zucchinis and leeks to the skillet. Sauté until softened.
- Season with salt, black pepper, and dried thyme. Cook for an additional 2-3 minutes.

For the Crème Fraîche Drizzle:

Make Crème Fraîche Drizzle:
- In a bowl, mix together vegan crème fraîche, minced garlic, fresh lemon juice, salt, and black pepper.

Assembling the Pizza:

Assemble Pizza:
- Once the pizza crust is baked and cooled, spread the sautéed zucchini and leek mixture over the crust.

Drizzle with Crème Fraîche:
- Drizzle the crème fraîche mixture over the zucchini and leek.

Sprinkle Cheese:
- Sprinkle shredded Emmental or Gruyere cheese over the pizza.

Bake:
- Return the pizza to the oven and bake for an additional 8-10 minutes, or until the cheese is melted and bubbly.

Additional Garnish:

Garnish:
- Garnish the German-style Zucchini and Leek Pizza with chopped fresh parsley and lemon zest.

Serve:
- Slice the pizza into portions and serve hot.

Enjoy the delicious flavors of zucchini and leek with a German twist on your pizza! Adjust toppings and seasonings according to your taste.

Vegan Black Forest Pizza

Ingredients:

For the Pizza Dough:

- 1 pizza dough (store-bought or homemade)

For the Chocolate Cherry Sauce:

- 1 cup frozen dark sweet cherries, pitted
- 2 tablespoons maple syrup
- 2 tablespoons cocoa powder
- 1/2 teaspoon vanilla extract
- Pinch of salt

For the Vegan Cream Cheese Drizzle:

- 1/2 cup vegan cream cheese, softened
- 2 tablespoons powdered sugar
- 1/2 teaspoon vanilla extract

For Toppings:

- 1/2 cup vegan dark chocolate, chopped or chocolate chips
- 1/4 cup sliced almonds, toasted
- Fresh cherries, pitted and halved

Additional Garnish:

- Vegan whipped cream (optional)
- Mint leaves for decoration

Instructions:

For the Pizza Dough:

	Preheat Oven:
		- Preheat your oven according to the pizza dough package instructions.
	Roll Out Pizza Dough:
		- Roll out the pizza dough on a floured surface to your desired thickness.
	Bake Pizza Dough:
		- Place the rolled-out dough on a pizza stone or baking sheet.

- Follow the pizza dough package instructions for baking. Typically, bake until the crust is golden brown.

For the Chocolate Cherry Sauce:

Prepare Chocolate Cherry Sauce:
- In a blender, combine frozen dark sweet cherries, maple syrup, cocoa powder, vanilla extract, and a pinch of salt.
- Blend until smooth.

For the Vegan Cream Cheese Drizzle:

Make Vegan Cream Cheese Drizzle:
- In a bowl, mix together softened vegan cream cheese, powdered sugar, and vanilla extract until smooth.

Assembling the Pizza:

Assemble Pizza:
- Once the pizza crust is baked and cooled, spread the chocolate cherry sauce over the crust.

Drizzle with Cream Cheese:
- Drizzle the vegan cream cheese mixture over the chocolate cherry sauce.

Add Toppings:
- Sprinkle chopped vegan dark chocolate or chocolate chips over the pizza.
- Add toasted sliced almonds and fresh cherries on top.

Bake:
- Return the pizza to the oven and bake for an additional 5-7 minutes, or until the toppings are heated through.

Additional Garnish:

Garnish:
- Optionally, garnish the Vegan Black Forest Pizza with vegan whipped cream, mint leaves, or additional fresh cherries.

Serve:
- Slice the pizza into portions and serve hot.

Enjoy the delightful combination of chocolate, cherries, and cream cheese in this Vegan Black Forest Pizza! Adjust toppings and sweetness according to your taste.

Vegan Kartoffelsuppe Pizza

Ingredients:

For the Pizza Dough:

- 1 pizza dough (store-bought or homemade)

For the Potato Leek Soup Base:

- 2 large potatoes, peeled and thinly sliced
- 1 leek, washed and thinly sliced
- 1 small onion, finely chopped
- 2 cloves garlic, minced
- 4 cups vegetable broth
- 1 cup unsweetened plant-based milk (e.g., almond, soy, or oat)
- 2 tablespoons olive oil
- Salt and black pepper to taste
- 1 teaspoon dried thyme
- 1 bay leaf

For Toppings:

- 1 cup vegan cheese (cheddar or mozzarella), shredded
- 1/4 cup chives, chopped
- Salt and black pepper to taste

Additional Garnish:

- Vegan sour cream or cashew cream
- Fresh parsley, chopped

Instructions:

For the Pizza Dough:

Preheat Oven:
- Preheat your oven according to the pizza dough package instructions.

Roll Out Pizza Dough:
- Roll out the pizza dough on a floured surface to your desired thickness.

Bake Pizza Dough:
- Place the rolled-out dough on a pizza stone or baking sheet.

- Follow the pizza dough package instructions for baking. Typically, bake until the crust is golden brown.

For the Potato Leek Soup Base:

Prepare Potato Leek Soup Base:
- In a large pot, heat olive oil over medium heat. Add chopped onions and minced garlic. Sauté until softened.

Add Potatoes and Leeks:
- Add thinly sliced potatoes, sliced leeks, dried thyme, bay leaf, salt, and black pepper to the pot. Stir well.

Cook Potatoes:
- Pour in vegetable broth and plant-based milk. Bring to a simmer and cook until the potatoes are tender.

Blend Soup Base:
- Remove the bay leaf and use an immersion blender to blend the soup until smooth. Adjust seasoning if needed.

Assembling the Pizza:

Assemble Pizza:
- Once the pizza crust is baked and cooled, spread the potato leek soup base over the crust.

Add Vegan Cheese:
- Sprinkle shredded vegan cheese over the pizza.

Season and Garnish:
- Season with additional salt and black pepper to taste.
- Sprinkle chopped chives over the pizza.

Bake:
- Return the pizza to the oven and bake for an additional 5-7 minutes, or until the vegan cheese is melted and bubbly.

Additional Garnish:

Garnish:
- Garnish the Vegan Kartoffelsuppe Pizza with dollops of vegan sour cream or cashew cream and chopped fresh parsley.

Serve:
- Slice the pizza into portions and serve hot.

Enjoy the comforting flavors of Kartoffelsuppe in a unique pizza form! Adjust toppings and seasonings according to your taste.

Vegan Rösti Pizza

Ingredients:

For the Pizza Dough:

- 1 pizza dough (store-bought or homemade)

For the Rösti Topping:

- 4 medium-sized potatoes, peeled and grated
- 1 small onion, finely chopped
- 2 tablespoons olive oil
- Salt and black pepper to taste
- 1 teaspoon dried thyme

For the Vegan Sour Cream Drizzle:

- 1 cup vegan sour cream
- 1 tablespoon lemon juice
- 1 tablespoon chopped fresh dill
- Salt to taste

Additional Toppings:

- 1 cup vegan cheese (cheddar or mozzarella), shredded
- 1/4 cup chives, chopped
- Optional: Vegan bacon bits or tempeh bacon crumbles

Additional Garnish:

- Fresh chives, chopped

Instructions:

For the Pizza Dough:

Preheat Oven:
- Preheat your oven according to the pizza dough package instructions.

Roll Out Pizza Dough:
- Roll out the pizza dough on a floured surface to your desired thickness.

Bake Pizza Dough:
- Place the rolled-out dough on a pizza stone or baking sheet.

- Follow the pizza dough package instructions for baking. Typically, bake until the crust is golden brown.

For the Rösti Topping:

Prepare Rösti Mixture:
- Grate the peeled potatoes and place them in a clean kitchen towel. Squeeze out excess moisture.
- In a bowl, mix the grated potatoes with chopped onions, olive oil, salt, black pepper, and dried thyme.

Cook Rösti:
- Heat a non-stick skillet over medium heat. Press the potato mixture into the skillet to form a round shape, creating a large hash brown. Cook until golden brown on both sides. Set aside.

For the Vegan Sour Cream Drizzle:

Make Vegan Sour Cream Drizzle:
- In a bowl, whisk together vegan sour cream, lemon juice, chopped fresh dill, and salt. Adjust the seasoning to taste.

Assembling the Pizza:

Assemble Pizza:
- Once the pizza crust is baked and cooled, place the cooked Rösti on top of the crust.

Add Vegan Cheese:
- Sprinkle shredded vegan cheese over the Rösti.

Drizzle with Sour Cream:
- Drizzle the vegan sour cream mixture over the pizza.

Add Toppings:
- Sprinkle chopped chives over the pizza.
- If desired, add vegan bacon bits or tempeh bacon crumbles.

Bake:
- Return the pizza to the oven and bake for an additional 5-7 minutes, or until the vegan cheese is melted and bubbly.

Additional Garnish:

Garnish:
- Garnish the Vegan Rösti Pizza with additional chopped fresh chives.

Serve:
- Slice the pizza into portions and serve hot.

Enjoy the flavors of crispy Rösti with a vegan twist in pizza form! Customize with your favorite toppings and seasonings.

Vegan Apfelkuchen (Apple Cake) Dessert Pizza

Ingredients:

For the Pizza Dough:

- 1 pizza dough (store-bought or homemade)

For the Apple Topping:

- 3 medium-sized apples, peeled, cored, and thinly sliced
- 2 tablespoons lemon juice
- 2 tablespoons vegan butter
- 3 tablespoons maple syrup or agave nectar
- 1 teaspoon ground cinnamon
- 1/4 teaspoon ground nutmeg
- Pinch of salt

For the Streusel Topping:

- 1/2 cup all-purpose flour
- 1/4 cup brown sugar
- 1/4 cup vegan butter, softened
- 1/2 teaspoon ground cinnamon

For the Glaze:

- 1/2 cup powdered sugar
- 1-2 tablespoons plant-based milk
- 1/2 teaspoon vanilla extract

Additional Garnish:

- Chopped nuts (e.g., walnuts or pecans), optional

Instructions:

For the Pizza Dough:

Preheat Oven:
- Preheat your oven according to the pizza dough package instructions.

Roll Out Pizza Dough:
- Roll out the pizza dough on a floured surface to your desired thickness.

Bake Pizza Dough:
- Place the rolled-out dough on a pizza stone or baking sheet.
- Follow the pizza dough package instructions for baking. Typically, bake until the crust is golden brown.

For the Apple Topping:

Prepare Apples:
- In a bowl, toss thinly sliced apples with lemon juice to prevent browning.

Cook Apple Mixture:
- In a skillet, melt vegan butter over medium heat. Add sliced apples, maple syrup or agave nectar, ground cinnamon, ground nutmeg, and a pinch of salt.
- Cook until the apples are softened and coated in the syrup, about 5-7 minutes. Set aside.

For the Streusel Topping:

Make Streusel Topping:
- In a bowl, combine all-purpose flour, brown sugar, softened vegan butter, and ground cinnamon. Mix with a fork until crumbly.

Assembling the Pizza:

Assemble Pizza:
- Once the pizza crust is baked and cooled, arrange the cooked apple slices evenly over the crust.

Sprinkle Streusel Topping:
- Sprinkle the streusel topping over the apple slices.

Bake:
- Return the pizza to the oven and bake for an additional 8-10 minutes, or until the streusel is golden brown.

For the Glaze:

Prepare Glaze:
- In a small bowl, whisk together powdered sugar, plant-based milk, and vanilla extract until smooth.

Additional Garnish:

Drizzle Glaze:

- Drizzle the glaze over the warm dessert pizza.

Garnish:
- Optionally, sprinkle chopped nuts over the glaze for added texture.

Serve:
- Slice the Vegan Apfelkuchen Dessert Pizza into portions and serve warm.

Enjoy this delicious and sweet dessert pizza with the flavors of traditional Apfelkuchen! Adjust sweetness and toppings according to your preference.

Vegan Sauerkraut and Potato Pizza

Ingredients:

For the Pizza Dough:

- 1 pizza dough (store-bought or homemade)

For the Sauerkraut and Potato Topping:

- 2 medium-sized potatoes, peeled and thinly sliced
- 1 cup sauerkraut, drained
- 1 small onion, thinly sliced
- 2 tablespoons olive oil
- Salt and black pepper to taste
- 1 teaspoon caraway seeds (optional)
- 1/4 cup vegan mayonnaise or vegan sour cream

Additional Toppings:

- 1 cup vegan cheese (cheddar or mozzarella), shredded
- Chopped fresh parsley for garnish

Instructions:

For the Pizza Dough:

Preheat Oven:
- Preheat your oven according to the pizza dough package instructions.

Roll Out Pizza Dough:
- Roll out the pizza dough on a floured surface to your desired thickness.

Bake Pizza Dough:
- Place the rolled-out dough on a pizza stone or baking sheet.
- Follow the pizza dough package instructions for baking. Typically, bake until the crust is golden brown.

For the Sauerkraut and Potato Topping:

Prepare Potatoes:
- In a skillet, heat olive oil over medium heat. Add thinly sliced potatoes and sauté until they start to soften.

Add Onions and Sauerkraut:

- Add thinly sliced onions to the skillet and continue to sauté until the onions are translucent.
- Add drained sauerkraut to the skillet and mix well. Cook for an additional 2-3 minutes.

Seasoning:
- Season the mixture with salt, black pepper, and caraway seeds (if using). Adjust to taste.

Assemble Pizza:
- Once the pizza crust is baked and cooled, spread the sauerkraut and potato mixture evenly over the crust.

Additional Toppings:

Add Vegan Cheese:
- Sprinkle shredded vegan cheese over the sauerkraut and potato mixture.

Bake:
- Return the pizza to the oven and bake for an additional 8-10 minutes, or until the vegan cheese is melted and bubbly.

Serving:

Drizzle Vegan Mayo or Sour Cream:
- Drizzle vegan mayonnaise or vegan sour cream over the hot pizza.

Garnish:
- Sprinkle chopped fresh parsley over the pizza for a burst of freshness.

Slice and Serve:
- Slice the Vegan Sauerkraut and Potato Pizza into portions and serve hot.

Enjoy the unique and savory flavors of sauerkraut and potatoes on your vegan pizza! Adjust toppings and seasonings according to your taste.

Vegan Schwarzwälder Kirschtorte Pizza

Ingredients:

For the Pizza Dough:

- 1 pizza dough (store-bought or homemade)

For the Cherry Compote:

- 2 cups fresh or frozen cherries, pitted
- 1/4 cup granulated sugar
- 1 tablespoon cornstarch
- 1 tablespoon water

For the Vegan Whipped Cream:

- 1 can (14 oz) coconut cream, chilled overnight
- 1/4 cup powdered sugar
- 1 teaspoon vanilla extract

For Chocolate Drizzle:

- 1/2 cup vegan dark chocolate, chopped
- 2 tablespoons coconut oil

Additional Garnish:

- Vegan chocolate shavings
- Maraschino cherries

Instructions:

For the Pizza Dough:

    Preheat Oven:
- Preheat your oven according to the pizza dough package instructions.

    Roll Out Pizza Dough:
- Roll out the pizza dough on a floured surface to your desired thickness.

    Bake Pizza Dough:
- Place the rolled-out dough on a pizza stone or baking sheet.
- Follow the pizza dough package instructions for baking. Typically, bake until the crust is golden brown.

For the Cherry Compote:

Prepare Cherry Compote:
- In a saucepan, combine pitted cherries, granulated sugar, cornstarch, and water.
- Cook over medium heat until the mixture thickens and the cherries release their juices. Set aside to cool.

For the Vegan Whipped Cream:

Make Vegan Whipped Cream:
- Scoop the solid part of the chilled coconut cream into a bowl (leave the liquid behind).
- Whip the coconut cream with powdered sugar and vanilla extract until stiff peaks form.

For the Chocolate Drizzle:

Prepare Chocolate Drizzle:
- In a heatproof bowl, melt vegan dark chocolate and coconut oil together. Stir until smooth.

Assembling the Pizza:

Assemble Pizza:
- Once the pizza crust is baked and cooled, spread a layer of the cherry compote over the crust.

Add Vegan Whipped Cream:
- Dollop the vegan whipped cream over the cherry compote.

Drizzle with Chocolate:
- Drizzle the melted chocolate over the pizza.

Additional Garnish:

Sprinkle Chocolate Shavings:
- Sprinkle vegan chocolate shavings over the pizza.

Add Maraschino Cherries:
- Garnish with maraschino cherries for a classic Black Forest Cake look.

Slice and Serve:
- Slice the Vegan Schwarzwälder Kirschtorte Pizza into portions and serve.

Enjoy the decadence of a Black Forest Cake in a unique pizza form! Adjust sweetness and toppings according to your preference.

www.ingramcontent.com/pod-product-compliance
Lightning Source LLC
LaVergne TN
LVHW081558060526
838201LV00054B/1947